TRIBAL ADMINISTRATION AND DEVELOPMENT

About the Author

Dr. S.G. Deogaonkar is a scholar of repute and his specialisation is Political and Social Anthropology, Tribal Development and Constitutional Law. He has been associated with developmental activities in tribal areas and completed many research projects based on field-research. He has participated and presented papers at many State and National level conferences including the Xth International Congress of Anthropological and Ethnological Sciences. He was a Member on the District Planning and Development Council of the Chandrapur district and was Chancellor's Nominee on the Nagpur University Senate. Dr. Deogaonkar was a Member-Participant of the Socio-Economic Groups on Scheduled Castes and Scheduled Tribes for formulation of the Eighth Five-Year Plan Schemes constituted under the Backward Classes Division of the Planning Commission. At present he is a Non-official Member on the Governing Body of the tribal Research and Training Institute of the Maharashtra State at Pune. He is also a Member of the School Council of the School of Humanities and Social Sciences of the Yashwantrao Chavan Maharashtra Open University at Nasik.

Dr. Deogaonkar has completed many post-doctor al research projects for the U.G.C. and ICSSR and was a National (post-doctoral) Research Fellow in Tribal Development of the Ministry of Welfare Government of India.

He has published many works which include, *Administration for Rural Development in India; The Madia of Bhamragud; Problems of Development of Tribal Areas; The Hill Korwa; The Korku Tribals; The Banjara; Political Anthropology; Tribal Eploitation; Tribal Development Plans* ete. He has also contributed four ethnographic notes to the 'People of Indha' compendium Published by the Anthropological Survey ot India.

Dr. Deogaonkar is working as Head, Department of Political Science at the Anand Niketan College, Warora (Maharashtra).

TRIBAL ADMINISTRATION AND DEVELOPMENT

(With Ethnographic Profiles of Selected Tribes)

S.G. DEOGAONKAR
Head, Department of Political Science
Anand Niketan College
Warora (Maharashtra)

CONCEPT PUBLISHING COMPANY PVT. LTD.
NEW DELHI-110059

ISBN: 978-81-7022-534-8

Edition 2025

Published and Printed by

Since 1974

Concept Publishing Company Pvt. Ltd.
A/15-16, Commercial Block, Mohan Garden,
New Delhi-110059 (India)
T : 91-11-41101460
E : publishing@conceptpub.com, *W*: www.conceptpub.com

PREFACE

It gives me great pleasure to place this book before teachers, scholars, administrators and social workers. Numerous schemes have been planned for the development of tribal populations in India since Independence.

Planned efforts have also been made and innovative structures and institutions have been created with a view to bring about a desired change in the life of our tribal people. An elaborate administrative organization and processes are being tried for attaining success in tribal development. The job for the administration has been more challenging in the area of tribal development as compared to that in other non-tribal rural areas and hence different experiments in approach and methods had to be tried based on the feed-back of earlier efforts.

The book tries to trace the development of the administrative measures for tribal development, right from the beginning up to the time of the Eighth Five-Year Plan. Different approaches to tribal development, the organizational set-up adopted and changes incorporated after intervals have also been described. An evaluatory discussion of all those measures has also been interrelated as and where possible.

The concept of development has been discussed and its nexus with tribal culture is also outlined. Issues related to personnel policy for tribal development administration also finds a place in the discussion.

Ethnographic profiles of four tribes representing different major tribal groups are given in a separate chapter.

The methods and constraints encountered while working in the tribal areas also form a part of the book. The analysis is based on the experience obtained from actual field work in tribal areas both from social service and academic research. Apart from my own work in this field, I have also drawn upon the experience and analysis of stalwarts in the field of tribal development, particularly late L.P.Vidyarthi, Dr. B.D. Sharma, Dr. B.K. Roy Burman, and a few others. The author expresses a deep sense of gratitude to all of them. I must also thank my wife, Dr (Mrs.) Shailaja Deogaonkar for her contribution.

My thanks are also due to Shri Ashok Kumar Mittal of the

Concept Publishing Company, New Delhi, for encouraging me to write this book which, I trust, will be welcome by teachers, scholars, administrators and others concerned with the field of tribal development administration.

S.G. DEOGAONKAR

CONTENTS

1

GENESIS AND GROWTH OF TRIBAL ADMINISTRATION

THE TRIBAL populations are the aboriginal inhabitants of our country and are found in all parts of India. For centuries they have been living a simple life based on the natural environment and have developed culture patterns congenial to their physical and the consequent social environment. References to such tribal groups and populations are found even in the literature on the ancient period, right from the *Ramayana* and *Mahabharata* periods. Their social and economic systems were in primordial forms and even the political institutions, though rudimentary and non-explicit, were present with definite roles and functions. Their traditional socio-economic and political institutions did have their impact on the later developments and the so-called tribal culture had cross-cultural exchanges with the other cultures.

Terminology

Different terms have been popularized by different authors for calling these groups. *Aborigines* or *Aboriginals* are the terms which connote that they were the first or original inhabitants of the land, having original habitat, native to the soil or indigenous.

While Risley, Grigson, Elwin, A.V. Thakkar prefer this term, Dr. Ghurye calls them "so-called" Aboriginies or Backward Hindus. The Hindi word *adivasi* is having the same connotation as *Aborigines*.

Hutton. calls them "Primitive Tribes". Some people, however, dislike the term aborigines or *Adivasi* and prefer the term *Vanavasi* (forest dwellers) or *Girijan* (mountain dwellers) which indicates the "nature" of their present habitat or that in the immediate past. The term "primitive" has also been used by different authors with different meanings. While some use it just to indicate tribal groups others use it to indicate a lower level of acculturation amongst tribal groups. Thus a primitive tribal group should mean a relatively more backward tribal group which is still nearer to its original cultural level.

The Government of India has recognized some tribal groups as being "primitive", and special plans as well as grants are sanctioned for their development. In Maharashtra State three Tribal groups are recognized as "primitive," namely, Madia-Gonds from Gadchiroli district, Kolams from Yovetmal district and Kinwat and Katkaris from Thane district.

Classification or Division of Tribal Population in India

For the sake of convenience and study the tribal people of India have been broadly classified on different bases.

Geographical or regional distribution forms the first base. On this basis the following five regions are considered.

(1) *North-Eastern Region*: It consists of Assam, Arunachal Pradesh, Mizoram, Nagaland and Tripura. The tribes in this region include the Garo, Kuki, Mizo, Khasi, Munda, Sema, Nagas, Riyang, Miri, Apa-Tani, etc.
(2) *The Sub-Himalayan Region*: It includes north and north-west India, Himachal Pradesh, the major tribes being Gurjar, Gaddi, Theru, Jaunsari, etc.
(3) *The Central and East India*: It consists of West Bengal, Bihar, Orissa, Madhya Pradesh and Uttar Pradesh. The tribes covered are: Baiga, Bondo, Juang, Kol, Khond, Santhal, Uraon, Ho, Munda, Lepcha, Korwa, Bhils, Pahadiya, etc.
(4) *South India*: This includes the States of Tamil Nadu, Kerala, Andhra Pradesh and Karnataka. The main tribes included are the Tod, Kol, Kadar, Chenchu, Koya, Gonds, Cholanaiken, Gadaba etc.
(5) *Western India*: Includes Rajasthan, Gujarat and Maharashtra and the tribes included are the Bhils, Garasia, Gonds, Kolams, Pardhans, Korku, Koli, Thakar, Katkari, Warli, Pawra, Munda, Kol, Khond, Dubla, etc.

Classification Based on Language

Another classification is based on the language spoken which is assigned to various language groups. These are:

(1) *Austric Language Group*: The tribes speaking languages from this group include Kol, Munda, Khasi, Nikobari, Korku, Santhals, Gadaba, etc.
(2) *Tibeto-Chinese Language Group*: For examples the Naga, Khasi, Kuki, Miri, Mizo, etc.
(3) *The Dravidian Language Group*: The Gond, Toda, Kolam, Koya, Pardhan, Uraon, etc.
(4) *The Indo-Europeon Language Group*: The Bhils, Warlis, Thakurs, Koli, etc.

Classification Based on Ethnic Roots

One more classification is based on the ethnic roots of the tribes. The more predominant are:

(1) *The Mongoloid Origin*: The Nagas, Mizo, Sema, Jaunsari, Apa-Tanis, Tharu, etc.
(2) *Proto-Austroloid*: This group usually speaks the so-called Kherwarian or Kaularian languages and includes the Munda, Ho, Bhils, Pahadia, Korku, Korwa, Baiga, Gonds, etc.
(3) *The Negrito*: Whom we usually recognize as being of Dravidian origin and include Toda, Kota, etc.

According to another usage the tribes from the South, like the Gonds, Kolam, Toda, Koya, etc., are called Dravidian in origin though they are considered a part of the Austroloid group. Herbert Rislay has also mentioned Indo-Aryan, Aryo-Dravidian, Mongolo-Dravidian, Sitho-Dravidian and Turki-Iranian as mixed ethnic roots.

Among the numerically most important tribes in India are the Gonds of Madhya Pradesh, Maharashtra and Andhra Pradesh and include the Koiturs, Koyas, Marhia/Madiya, Murhias, Raj-Gonds, Pardhans, Dhurve, Khatulwars, Parajas.

The second largest group of tribals includes those tribes

described as Kaularian tribes and include the Santhals, Munda and Ho spread over in Bihar, Orissa and West Bengal as well as the Bhils and Korwas from Rajasthan, Gujarat and the Korkus in Madhya Pradesh and Maharashtra. This group speaks the "so-called" Kherwarian or the Kaularian group of languages which includes the Munda group of dialects, and are supposed to be of pre-Dravidian origin.

G.A. Grierson in his *Linguistic Survey of India*, Vol. IV (*Munda and Dravidian Languages*) (First Reprint 1967) gives references hinting at links between the Munda and Dravidian group of languages (pp. 167-182). Hodgson classed the languages under the head of Tamulian. Ho, Santhali, Bhumji, Kurakh and Mundari (all from Munda family) were considered as dialects of Kol languages. Logan also followed Hodgson and called them as North Dravidian. Grierson quotes Max Muller stating, ". . . I can see many coincidences between Uraon, Rajmahali and Gondi on the one side and Sinbhum, Santhal, Bhamji and Mundala words on the other. . ., Both are two different races. . . came in contact in these regions. . . with ethnic name 'Munda'." This analysis helps us in understanding that there were cultural contacts amongst the tribal groups which are dispersed in different parts and are assigned different ethnic origins and dialects. The similarities in many cultural traits found in distant tribal groups in India can be interpreted on this basis.

Paternalistic Mode of Administration

The system of administration specially of tribal areas during the British regime can be described as paternalistic in mode and depended largely on the personal qualities of the administrator, his character, initiative and vigour. Military officers were preferred to civilian officers for administering the tribal areas which were known as Non-Regulation Provinces. This was not only because of their efficiency but also due to their capacity to suppress the unrest or tribal rebellion if required. Blunt who had experience of tribal administration of civil justice in Arracan in 1828 and later became a member of the Governor General's Council was followed by Wilkinson and Dent who worked as Special Commissioners for suppressing the Great Kole Rising of 1832. Wilkinson had direct experience of running administration in the tribal areas of Nagpur for more than a decade and was influenced with the ideals of administration of relief. In Chota-Nagpur during 1834 when Wilkinson's rules were promulgated and even during 1855 when a separate Santhal Parganas District under the Yule Regulation was created the British policy for these Non-Regulation Areas still remained isolationistic in nature.

During the 19th century there were tribal rebellions in many areas which compelled the Government to think of and apply legislative and executive measures in these areas. An adjunct of the policy was induction of the Christian Missionaries in the tribal areas. In 1874 the Scheduled Distrit Act was passed and when the Government of India Acts of 1909 and 1935 were passed, the tribal areas from various States were excluded from the purview of the legislature, as "Partially Excluded Areas and Excluded Areas". Thus isolation of the areas and the paternal despotism of the administration were continued and the government felt that this would help in supressing tribal rebellions and weaning them away from the national movements.

When national leaders and Mahatma Gandhi gave a call to the nation, the tribal leaders from many areas responded, for example, in Bihar the Tana Bhagat Movement cooperated with the Non-coöperation movement launched by Gandhi and participated in agitations like the Flag Satyagraha at Nagpur. Due to this coming together the national leaders could understand the conditions and problems of the tribal population and became aware of the need of integrating the tribal people with the mainstream of Indian life. Social workers such as Shri A.V. Thakkar of the Servants of India Society started pioneering work among the tribal people and this helped in creating new attitudes and approach in the minds of national leaders towards the tribal population. Even some British officers who had studied tribes and created a vast literature such as Dalton, Risley, Haton, Grikson, Grierson and later Dr. Elwin or missionaries such as Hislop, and others helped in giving a new direction to the administration of tribal areas.

After independence the Constituent Assembly appointed a sub-committee for the "Excluded areas and Partially Excluded Areas (other than Assam)" with Shri A.V. Thakkar (Thakkar Bappa) as Chairman, thus demonstrating its responsibility towards the tribal people. Sardar Patel also advocated that every tribal must reach a high level. All these efforts were reflected in the Constitution of India which provided different safeguards for the welfare of about

427 scheduled tribe communities numbering 38.2 millions at the commencement of the First Five Year Plan (as per the Census of India, 1971). Later, planned development concentrated on tribal development starting with the First Five Year Plan and went on innovating new structures and models with sufficient financial outlays for tribal development.

Constitutional Safeguards for Tribal Population

Definition of a Tribe

For long, solution to the problem of definition of a tribe has been eluding the administration. Anthropologists and sociologists have attempted different definitions.

W.J. Perry difines tribe as a group speaking a common dialect and inhabiting a common territory.

Bogardus defines tribe as a tribal group based on the need for protection, on ties of blood-relationships and on the strength of a common religion.

Gillin and Gillin consider any collection of pre-literate local group which occupies a common general territory, speaks a common language and practises a common culture as a tribe.

D.N. Majumdar defines a tribe as a collection of families or groups of families bearing a common name, members of which occupy the same territory, speak the same language and observe certain taboos regarding marriage, profession or occupation and have developed a well-assessed system of reciprocity and mutuality of obligations.

Dr. Revers defines a tribe as a social group of a simple kind, the members of which speak a common dialect and act together for such common purposes as welfare.

The *Imperial Gazetteer* had defined a tribe as a collection of families bearing a common name, speaking a common dialect, occupying or professing to occupy a common territory and which is not usually endogamous, though originally it might have been.

Kamaladevi Chattopadhyaya defines a tribe as a social group usually with a definite area, dialect, cultural homogeneity, and unifying social organization. It can include several sub-groups.

Dictionary of Anthropology (E.B. Tylor) defines a tribe as a social group usually with a social area, dialect, cultural homogeneity and unifying social organization. It may include several sub-groups such as Sibs or villages. The tribe ordinarily has a leader and may have a common ancestor, as well as a patron deity. The families or small communities making up the tribe are linked through economic, social, religious, family or blood ties.

Funk and Wagnalls Standard Dictionary (Comprehensive International Edition) defines tribe as "a division, class or group of people, varying ethnologically according to circumstances from which their separation or distinction is supposed to originate", or "a group or aggregate of persons among primitive peoples, usually consanguineous and endogamous, under one chief, characterized by its own culture and having a name, a dialect, a government and usually a territory of its own".

This indicates that different authors have given importance to different aspects or characteristics and there is no universally accepted definition of a tribe. The International Labour Organization (ILO) in its Report of 1953 stated that, "there can be no standard which can apply to all indegenous or aboriginal groups throughout the world". However, a consensus may lead us to identify and define any group as a tribe which displays the following characteristics, viz.:

(i) a definite habitat and area,
(ii) a unified social organization based primarily on blood relationship (consanguinity),
(iii) cultural homogeneity,
(iv) a common scheme of deities and common ancestors, and
(v) a common dialect with a common folk-lore.

The above characteristics assume importance specially when anthropologists are faced with problems of development. Due to the process of acculturation which is always in action (though its pace may differ) some groups travel away from the original position and display slightly different characteristics from those of its original stalk. A relative estimate may become necessary when development schemes and the nature or types of benefits are being planned, administrators as well as anthropologists concerned with the process may have to face a situation in which it is incumbent to identify the status of a group, that is, whether it is a "tribe" or a tribal group or not and, secondly, whether it is at the same or different level of aculturation as that of the original or other similar tribal group or not.

Acculturation is the process by which a whole way of life is in a process of change under the influence of another culture. This cultural change may be slow or rapid and in due course it may lead to partial or even total assimilation with other cultures. Each tribal group may be at a different level of acculturation. On this basis depending upon the degree or level of acculturation tribal groups may be broadly classified as under:

"Primitive" tribal groups

These are at a very low level of acculturation. Their habitat is in inaccessible areas in forests, on mountains or valleys and are secluded, and still practise primitive agriculture usually described as *Zoom* or *Penda* or *Dahia*, i.e. shifting cultivation. Socially and/or economically they are still at the "primitive" stage, for example, the Madia/Marhia Gonds, the Katkaris from Maharashtra; the Cholanaikens from Neil mountains on the Kerala-Karnataka border, the Hill Korwas (Raigarh district) of Madhya Pradesh, the Bodo, the Baiga the Juang etc.

Acculturized Tribal Groups

These groups are slightly more acculturized and live in forest which are accessible.

Highly Acculturized Tribal Groups

These groups include those who have established contacts with the modern world and show a high level of acculturation. These groups have adopted many traits from the modern cultural stream, but still maintain their tribal characteristics and identity. For example, the Naga—particularly their sub-tribes like the Aao, the Gonds on the plains, the Korkus, the Bhils, etc.

Modernized Tribal Groups

These group's tribes are at a still higher level of acculturization, that is, they are modernized tribals who are almost assimilated in the modern cultural stream. Sections from the Santhals, Munda, Uraons reflect this stage. Some families or individuals from different tribal groups also come under this category.

As per the 1981 Census, the scheduled tribe population constitutes 7.76 per cent of India's total population.

Provisions in the Constitution

The Constitution of India contains many provisions for the protection and welfare of the tribal population. Article 46 mentions that the State is committed to the welfare of the scheduled castes and scheduled tribes and their protection from all types of socio-economic exploitation. It must strive for their development. However, even this or any other Article in our Constitution does not clearly define a "tribe". The President of India is empowered by Article 342 (i) to notify and specify any tribe/tribal community from any area as a "Scheduled Tribe". On such notification the tribe so specified is added to the List of Scheduled Tribes in the Fifth Schedule and is thus entitled to all the Constitutional safeguards and protection. So what seems to be *indirectly* defined is the concept of a *scheduled* tribe but not a "tribe". Article 366 specifies the meaning of Scheduled Tribes which means (Clause 25 of the Article), "such tribes or tribal communities or parts or groups within such tribes or tribal communities as are deemed to be Scheduled Tribes for the purpose of this Constitution."

Article 275 provides for special grants for tribal welfare from the Government of India to some States and forms part of the Sixth Schedule.

Article 164 makes it obligatory to appoint a Minister-in-charge of Tribal Welfare (who may, in addition be in-charge of the Scheduled Castes and Backward Classes) in the States of Bihar, Madhya Pradesh and Orissa. These three States are having the largest Scheduled tribes population in our Union followed by Maharashtra and Rajasthan, respectively.

Article 244 makes applicable the provisions of the Fifth Schedule to the administration and control of the Scheduled Areas and Scheduled Tribes in any State specified in Part A and Part B of the First Scheduled, other than the State of Assam. It also mentions that the provisions of the Sixth Schedule shall apply to the administration of the tribal areas in the State of Assam.

The Fifth Schedule makes provisions for establishment of Tribes Advisory Councils examining applicability of laws to the Scheduled Areas, delineation of boundary of the Scheduled Areas, and making amendment of the Schedule as such.

The Sixth Schedule makes provisions as to the administration of Tribal Areas of Assam by setting up Autonomous Districts and Autonomous Regions and constituting Distirct Councils and Regional Councils. It also specifies powers of the District Councils and Regional Councils to make laws and administration of justice in the Autonomous Districts and Autonomous Regions. The Schedule also makes provisions for delineation of (1) executive powers of the District Council, (2) District and Regional Funds, (3) powers to assess and collect land revenue and to impose taxes, (4) licences or leases for the purpose of prospecting for extraction of minerals, (5) powers of the District Council to make regulations for the control of money-lending and trading by non-tribals, (6) publication of laws, and regulations made under the Schedule, (7) application of Acts of Parliament and Legislature of the State to Autonomous Districts and Autonomous Regions, (8) estimated receipts and expenditure pertaining to Autonomous Districts to be shown separately in the annual financial statement, (9) appointment of a commission to inquire into and report on the administration of Autonomous Districts and Autonomous Regions, (10) annulment or suspension of Acts and Resolutions of District and Regional Councils, (11) dissolution of a District or a Regional Council, (12) exclusion of areas from a Autonomous District in forming constituencies in such districts, (13) application of the provisions of this Schedule to areas elsewhere such as the North-East Frontier Tract including Balipara Frontier Tract, Tirap Frontier Tract, Abor Hills District, and Misimi Hills District, (14) transitional provisions until the constitution of a District Council and (15) tribal areas of Assam.

Articles 330/331 of the Constitution make special provision for reservation of seats for (a) Scheduled-Castes (b) Scheduled Tribes in the Lok Sabha and Legislative Assemblies of States, except the Scheduled Tribes in the tribal areas of Assam and in the Autonomous District of Assam.

Seats are to be reserved also for the Autonomous Districts in the Legislative Assembly of the State of Assam.

Such reservation must be in the proportions of the Scheduled Tribe population in that State to the total population of the State.

Article 335 seeks reservation of posts in public services of the Union and States for the Scheduled Caste/Scheduled Tribe population but this must be consistent with the maintenance of efficiency of administration.

Both the above reservations were initially meant for 10 years since the commencement of the Constitution (Article 334) but the provision has been amended after every 10 years extending the period by 10 years every time.

With a view to ensuring the supervision and control of the Union Government, Article 338 provides for the appointment of a special officer for the Scheduled Castes and Scheduled Tribes; and also specifies his duties as to investigate all matters relating to the safeguards provided to them. The President of India appoints this officer, who submits his reports before both Houses of Parliament. The Commissioner for Scheduled Castes and Scheduled Tribes has been functioning as per the provisions of this Article and his scope includes States as well as Union Territories.

Article 339 outlines the control of the Union over the administration of the Scheduled Areas and Welfare of Scheduled Tribes. Under the provisions of this Article the President may appoint any time and shall at the expiration of 10 years from the commencement of this Constitution a Commission to report on the administration of the Scheduled Areas and the Welfare of the Scheduled Tribes. A National Commission for Scheduled Castes and Scheduled Tribes has since been appointed (since 1990 with Shri Ram Dhan, M.P., as its first Chairman). Under this Article the Union is empowered to give directions to any State in regard to drawing up and execution of schemes specified in the direction and essential for the welfare of the Scheduled Tribes in the State.

Fundamental Rights and Directive Principles

The Fundamental Rights in Part III of the Constitution and the Directive Principles of State Policy in Part IV of the Constitution also contain general as well as some specific provisions which safeguard and further the interests of the Scheduled Castes and Scheduled Tribes.

Articles 14 to 35 contain rights which have a bearing on the interests of the Scheduled Tribes. Right to Equality, Right to Freedom, Right Against Exploitation, Right to Education and

Culture safeguard the interests and protect the rights of all citizens. However, certain exceptions and subsequent amendments to some Articles are specifically meant to protect the interests of the Scheduled Tribes. An example can be cited of the Right to Equality. It prohibits discrimination on grounds of religion, race, caste, sex, place of birth, etc., which is a positive benefit to the hitherto discriminated against people from the Scheduled Caste/Tribe population. However, the same Article assured equality of opportunity in matters of public employment (Article 16). But after suitable amendment to Article 16 (4) was introduced to provide for reservations in appointment to backward classes of India if, "in the opinion of the State, they are not adequately represented in the services under the State." (First Amendment in 1951).

Article 17 abolishes untouchability in unequivocal terms and declares it forbidden and an offence punishable in accordance with the law. This too has conferred a direct benefit and helped in social upgradation.

Article 23 confers a right against exploitation and ends exploitation in all froms. Thus it prohibits traffic in human beings and forced labour like *begar* and prohibits discrimination on grounds of race, caste, class, etc., while imposing compulsory service for public purposes only. Consequently, members of the Scheduled Castes and Scheduled Tribes who were subjected to different forms of bonded labour got emancipation due to this right.

Article 25 which assures freedom of conscience and free profession, practice and propogation of one's own religion and faith to all its citizens went a long way in assuring the tribal population that their tradition and culture in matters of faith and workship would continue.

The cultural and educational right enshrined in Article 29 assures not only right to get education and admission to such educational institutions maintained by the State or aided by the State, but also to conserve and develop their distinct language, script or culture. This does protect the interests of minorities including the tribals.

All other rights also contributed in the protection of the interests of the Scheduled Tribes along with and also vis-a-vis other citizens. The right to constitutional remedies is the statutory instrument for the protection and justiciability of these rights.

The Directive Principles of State Policy, though not justiciable like the Fundamental Rights, guided the formulation of public policy and legislation at the Union and State levels and as such the social and economic principles meant for removing or reducing economic inequalities, assuring minimum wage and social security, particularly the safeguards against expliutation of women and children provisions for employment guarantee, conservation of the labour capacities, etc., helped the weaker sections in general and the scheduled castes and scheduled tribes in particular by sponsoring and giving a fillip to social legislation. Though this took time, the goods were delivered. Free and compulsory education, health and hygiene awareness, help to pregnant and nursing mothers, free legal aid, etc., all contributed to furthering social welfare and establishment of an egalitarian society. The Preamble of our Constitution eulogizes lofty principles of Justice (social, economic and political), Equality and Fraternity. But unless these are translated into reality and enjoyed by the poor and hitherto exploited tribal people real development in its full sense would not be achieved.

The tribal communities constitute a large part of our national population. The percentage of tribal population to total population is given below as detailed in the Censes of India 1981.

Percentage of Scheduled Tribes Population
To Total Population (Census 1981)*

		Percentage
India	..	7.76
Islands or States/Territories in the North-East Hill region show the following percentage.		
Lakshadweep	..	93.82
Mizoram	..	93.55
Nagaland	..	83.99
Meghalaya	..	80.58
Dadra & Nagar Haveli	..	78.82
Arunachal Pradesh	..	69.82
Tripura	..	28.44
Manipur	..	27.30
Sikkim	..	23.27
States on the plains in the mainland with majority of non-tribal population show following concentrations.		
Madhya Pradesh	..	22.97
Orissa	..	22.43
Gujarat	..	14.22

Rajasthan	..	12.21
Maharashtra	..	9.19
Bihar	..	8.31
Andhra Pradesh	..	5.93

* *Source* : Census of India, 1981, Paper-2 of 1984, Statement-4; pp. 6-7

2

APPROACHES TO TRIBAL DEVELOPMENT

What is Development?

WE have attempted to understand the meaning and the scope of the word tribe. But since the planned efforts for development started scant attention has been paid to the meaning of the term development. The dictionary meaning of the word "develop" is to expand or to bring out the potentialities, capabilities or to cause to come to completeness or perfection, and 'development', gradual evolution or completion and the result of such an evolution or completion. When modern political analysts started concentration on area studies in developing countries such as India, Sri Lanka, Pakistan, Burma, Indonesia, Nigeria, Ghana, etc., a new concept of political development was evolved. Among others, Lucian Pie, David Apter, Winer, etc., elaborated the concept based on their field studies. Lucian Pie defined political development in terms of cultural diffusion and adopting, turning and adjusting old patterns of life to new ones. Coleman even thought of a development syndrome depending upon the level of three factors present in each developing country, viz.

(i) the principle of equality present behind the basic changes in population—awareness about such a principle and obedience to relevant laws;
(ii) the capacity of the political system for satisfying the demands, resolution of conflicts and governance of public affairs; and
(iii) the structural factors in the organization of the political system and the capacity to finely differentiate between

such factors.

A particular set of characteristics based on the above three factors gives rise to a particular development syndrome. Rostow considers four stages of the process of political development. These are:

(a) Concentration of political power in the State and, through it, political integration;
(b) Economic development through industrialization;
(c) National welfare through the political and economic power of the State with benefits to the people; and
(d) Abundance, upgradation of the material life of the people.

In developing countries like India, though the democratic model is adopted, it is inevitable that the "administration" which plans and administers development has the political power concentrated in it. Milton J. Esman says that throughout the developing world, the political system is the legitimate, order-maintaining or transferring system of society. This "political" element involves,[1]

(i) a "governing elite", that moves and guides the modernizing process;
(ii) a "doctrine" which legitimizes, in terms of programmed action, the norms, priorities, instruments and strategies of the governing elite; and
(iii) a series of instruments through which two-way communication is facilitated and through which commitments to action are translated into operating programmes.

Governing elites are defined by Esman in a functional sense as those who exercise major decision-making power in the national government. It includes both, those who hold formal positions of responsibility and those who are not formally in governmental hierarchy but exert important influence in decision-making being sympathetically associated with those in power. It is probably due to this reason that people tend to conceive development through administrative efforts as the only or chief means of applying the "doctrine" (or "formula"?) of changing the forms and norms of communities. This brings in another malady which, unfortunately, has been inherent in India since the Community Development Programme started. Though it was envisaged to be a "people's" movement, it only remained a governmental programme sans people's initiative. This was more so in tribal areas due to poverty, ignorance, culture gap and absence of development oriented leadership. Once it became bureaucratic achievement of physical targets in terms of amounts spent (as per budget heads) it became the criteria for estimating the success of the development programme.

J.D. Montgomery also says that development is conceived as an aspect of change that is desirable, broadly predicted or planned and administered or at least influenced by governmental action. The term is not used synonymously with "growth". In the developing countries of Asia, Africa and Latin America, development requires social and cultural change as well as economic growth, which have a reciprocal relationship. Hence development means change plus growth. From this point of view development of persons – men or women – in turn means *awareness*. Awareness includes self-awareness, awareness of what is going on within us and of the world around us; awareness of our own feelings and needs; awareness of the impact that the world around us has on us, and the impact that we have or could have on the world; and in this inter-action of the world as well as those blocking growth.[2]

Thus development work would be good if,

(a) the beneficiaries become increasingly aware of themselves and the world they live in, and especially of their capacity to transform it; and,
(b) the recipients are helped to remove obstacles to personal growth.

Thus our attitude towards development has to shift from a greater emphasis on economic development to a greater emphasis on personal growth.[3] It then becomes person-oriented than (physical) target-oriented. If self-respect and self-confidence are developed in one they would develop one's faith in oneself and fatalistic attitudes would change creating development-oriented attitudes. Thus development ultimately presupposes an attitudinal change towards new values, ideals, plans and programmes and these should be voluntarily accepted and adopted in such a way that the changed behaviour would continue even after the agent(s) for development leaves the area. This type of change is important but difficult so far as tribal populations are concerned. They are more ethnocentric in their attitudes and timid as well as suspicious (or cautious?) due to years of exploitative experience.

Different Approaches to Tribal Development

During the modern era the Government arms reached the hilly and forest tribal areas for the first time during the British regime. Till then some of the tribal areas had their own chiefs with a traditional pattern of political organization and others were stray scattered groups either ruled by other kings, Maharajas or were left to themselves as if in a "State of Nature". Right from the days of (1772) Warren Hastings, attempts to bring such bandit hill-men" like the Pahariyas of the Rajmahal hills under the "pale of civilization" were made but the administration was of a military and paternalistic type. It was obvious that the British Administration was not much concerned with the fate of these tribal populations as they did not influence the British interest in India and hence their isolation was continued during the British regime. Politically, these tribals were not significant for the administration and whatever interest in their society and culture was shown was by individual British administrators such as W.V. Grigson, Lucie Smith, R.V. Russel, Capt. Dalton and others who were either scholars/researchers or missionaries such as R.H. Lowie, W.C. MacLeod, Dr. Verrier Elwin, and others. But the policy of the British administration was apathetic towards the tribals and there was no attempt to develop them. The work done by Christian missionaries was totally on a different footing.

After Independence, planned development started and broadly three different approaches were advanced.

Policy of Isolation

The first approach was a legacy of the British regime, and is usually described as "leave them untouched". This was based on a policy of isolation and was justified on the grounds that their traditional culture ought to be preserved and hence there should be no interference by planners. It was also criticized by Thakkar Bappa (1941) that the anthropologists wanted them (the tribals) as "specimens in a zoo" so that their academic field-laboratories would always be available. Dr. Verrier Elwin's name was earlier associated with this approach, though, in fact, he was not an isolationist but advocated the preserving of the salient features of tribal culture.

Policy of Assimilation

Another diametrically opposite approach was the policy of assimilation of tribal culture and population in the mainstream of national life as early as possible. The advocates of this view even supported a direct assimilation without waiting for a slow and long-drawn changeover. Iravati Karve was one of its strong advocates.

Policy of Slow and Steady Assimilation

In between these directly opposing views was developed a moderate view which is usually recognized as Jawaharlal Nehru's view. This was a policy of slow and steady assimilation of tribal culture and life in the national mainstream without disturbing the healthy features of tribal life, and this change should be on their (tribal people's) own initiative and their willing consent.

The Report of the Study Team (1959) also endorsed this policy when it stated that "with the linking up of the tribal areas with the outside world, the question whether we should adopt a policy of assimilation or otherwise is no more than of mere academic interest."

At that stage Dr. Verrier Elwin agreed with Pandit Nehru that the policy of isolation of the tribals or leaving them untouched as "specimens in a human zoo" or a "national park" was out of the question. Dragging to the mainstream of an outside culture was also not advisable. Nehru said, "The Government of India is determined to help tribal people to grow according to their own genius and tradition." Respecting the tribal life and culture and to bring the best thing in modern life to them but in such a way that these will not destroy other traditional way of life but will activate and even attract them to a better and fuller life was the crux of the policy. Dr. Elwin very vividly and emphatically advocates Nehru's views when he says, "The tribesmen will be of greatest service to India if they are able to bring their own peculiar treasures into common life, not by becoming second-rate copies of ourselves. Their moral virtues, their self-reliance, their courage, their artistic gifts, their cheerfulness are the things we need."

The First Five Year Plan Draft outline gives official recognition to Nehru's views when it states,[4] "The conditions are now generally such that there has to be a positive policy of assisting the tribal people to develop their natural resources and to evolve a productive economic life wherein they will enjoy the fruits of their labour and will not be exploited by more organized economic forces from outside. So far as their religious and social life is concerned, it is not desirable to bring about changes except at the initiative of the tribal people themselves and with their willing consent. It is accepted that there are many healthy features of tribal life, which should be not only retained but developed. The qualities of their dialects, and the rich content of their arts and crafts also need to be appreciated and preserved."

Jawaharlal Nehru, in his Foreword to the second edition of Verrier Elwin's book, *A Philosophy for NEFA*, says,

> "We cannot allow matters to drift in the tribal areas or just not take interest in them. In the world of today that is not possible or desirable. At the same time we should avoid over-administering these areas and, in particular, sending too many outsiders into tribal territory."

It was thus between the two extreme positions that the middle approach was adopted. Development in various ways there has to be in the form of good communications, medical facilities, education and better agriculture. These avenues of development should, however, be pursued within the broad framework or the following five fundamental principles.

(i) People should develop along the lines of their own genius, we should avoid imposing anything on them. We should try to encourage in every way their own traditional arts and culture;

(ii) Tribal rights in land and forests should be respected;

(iii) We should try to train and build up a team of their own people to do the work of administration and development.

Some technical personnel from outside will, no doubt, be needed, especially in the beginning. But we should avoid introducing too many outsiders into tribal territory;

(iv) We should not over-administer these areas or overwhelm them with the multiplicity of schemes. We should rather work through and not in rivalary to their own social and cultural institutions; and

(v) We should judge results, not by statistics or the amount of money spent, but by the quality of human character that was evolved.

The First Five Year Plan had outlined a positive policy for tribal development as under.[5]

"There may be a good deal of justification for such (isolation) a policy of non-interference; but it is not easily practicable when tribal life has been influenced by social forces from without, and tribal communities have reached a certain degree of acculturization accompanied by the penetration of communications in the tribal areas, and of social services for the betterment of their lives." Taking into consideration the conditions of the tribal people the First Plan outlined a positive policy for assisting them as under:-

(1) Assisting them to develop their natural resources and to evoke a productive economic life wherein they will enjoy the fruits of their labour and will not be exploited by more organized economic forces from outside;

(2) It is not desirable to bring about changes in their religions and social life, except at the initiative of the tribal people themselves and with their willing consent;

(3) It is accepted that there are many healthy features in tribal life which should not only be retained but also developed; and

(4) The qualities of their dialects, and the rich content of their arts and crafts also need to be appreciated and preserved.

The Nehru approach to tribal development ultimately filters down to the following four commitments, viz.

(a) to preserve, strengthen and develop all that is best in the tribal society;

(b) to protect tribal economic rights;
(c) to unite and integrate the tribes in a true-heart unity with India as a whole, so that they may play a full part in her life; and
(d) to develop welfare and educational facilities so that every tribesman may have an equal opportunity with his fellow citizens on the open country and the plains.

REFERENCES

1. Esman, Miltan J., 1966, "The Politics of Development Administration", in *Approaches to Development—Politics, Administration and Change*. McGraw Book Hill, New York, 1966, p.259.
2. Montgomery, J.D., 1966, "A Royal invitation-Variation of three elastic theories:, in *Approaches to Development—Politics, Administration and Change*, McGraw Book Hill, New York, p.71.
3. Herodero, J.M., 1977, *Rural Development and Social Change*, Manohar Book Service, New Delhi, pp. 65-67.
4. G.O.I., Planning Commission, 1952, *First Five Year Plan*, New Delhi, pp. 636-640
5. *Ibid.*

3

POLICIES, PLANS AND PROGRAMMES FOR TRIBAL DEVELOPMENT

THE Community Development Blocks were expected to create a new thrust for development in the rural areas and engender a process of self-sustained growth. No aspect of community life, therefore, was kept outside the purview of this programme. Harmonious development of all facets of community life was envisaged as the main task in the programme. Thus, the programmes in C.D. Blocks covered a wide spectrum of activities in agriculture, animal husbandry, education, health, communications social services, rural industries, panchayats and so on. Since the socio-economic situation varies from one region to another and within the same region as well, a separate plan was to be prepared for each Block with reference to its resource potential and the problems faced by the community. Programme formulation was, therefore, to follow a reconnoitral survey of resources in close collaboration with the people. Block Advisory Committees and District Advisory Committees were constituted to ensure constant consultation with the people and pragmatic review of the programme.

The Community Development (CD) programme was comprehensive, and hence CD, concept was equally applicable to the tribal areas. The same principles of plan formulation and implementation could be applied to the tribal region and specific programmes could be moulded to their special needs. It was, however, realized in the very beginning that the task to be accomplished in the tribal areas was much more difficult. These areas are hilly with meagre communications and very little institutional infrastructure. This would require a much greater investment and personal attention of the extension workers. It was, therefore, decided to supplement the programme of Community Development in these areas. In 1954, following in the footprints of CD Project, 43 Special Multipurpose Tribal Development Blocks were started in the country. This programme was soon reviewed. It was realized that it would not be possible to start and sustain such an intensive programme all through the tribal region within a short period. A less intensive model of an ordinary Tribal Development Block was, therefore, evolved. The norm for the establishment of a Tribal Development Block was considerably smaller, both in terms of population and area coverage, compared to a Community Development Block. In the beginning, the tribal development blocks were taken up in areas having highest tribal concentration. All areas with more than two-thirds tribal population were covered by the end of the Third Five Year Plan. There were about five hundred Tribal Development Blocks on ground by that time covering about 40 per cent of the total tribal population. The programme, however, was not extended further geographically in the following years. Thus, tribal areas, which had more than 50 per cent tribal population but less than two-thirds, continued to be served by the general programme of development in the Community Development Blocks.

Although conceptually both the CD and TD Blocks were comprehensive and all-inclusive, in practice specific outlays were set apart for each area for a specific period. They gradually acquired a schematic form which also became quite rigid in due course. In the meantime, new departments were emerging both in the Central and State Governments as the need for greater attention to each activity was realized. These departments started preparing intensive programmes for their respective sectors at the macro level, but they paid little attention to the micro units. Each department was keen to achieve results opting for a best combination of resources, infrastructure and sociological factors, where necessary. The investments in the State and the Central plans grew from plan to plan and from year to year. The quantum of developmental effort under CD and TD Blocks remained constant but in relative terms shrank to a small proportion of the total national developmental effort. The programmes under agriculture, education and health particularly out stripped the narrow frame of CD and TD Blocks at a very early stage. Other activities were also gradually withdrawn leaving the Blocks with an impressive outer shell but with only a small content.

The massive developmental effort in the first two decades in our country had resulted in a sustained growth though not of the desired order. Food production, industrial potential and educational growth were recording a fast enough rate of growth. Yet the growing disparity between the different sections of the community even with the substantial rise in the Gross National Product was becoming clearer, particularly in the rural areas. The review showed that the rural development programmes in the first phase were largely land-based. Bulk of the land resources are owned by a small section in the rural community leaving large masses to subsist as small farmers or landless labourers. Even amongst those owning land, it was the articulate and better-off sections in the community who cornered the lion's share in the developmental plans. This was perhaps inevitable at least in the early years, since they were also the opinion leaders through whom it was necessary to pass the initial extension message in the rural area. This phase, however, could not be continued indefinitely. There could be no rational base for this approach when the economy as a whole became resilient and attention could be focused on distributive justice as well. In the Fourth Five Year Plan, a series of programmes, therefore, were conceived which were addressed to specific target groups. The Small Farmers' Development Agencies (SFDA) and Marginal Farmers and Agricultural Labourers Development Agencies (MFAL) were the first two in the series. In these cases, attention was shifted from area development to development of identified individuals who qualified for special attention according to certain objective criteria. The Drought Prone Areas Programme (DPAP) was another effort in the same direction though with a difference. Here the problem is faced by an entire region which is depressed because of its agro-climatic situation. The specific target-group approach, however, was adopted even here as far as possible. Greater attention was focused on the weaker sections of society. In the wake of establishment of these area specific and weaker-group oriented projects, the programmes for tribal areas were also intensified on a pilot basis. Tribal Development Agencies (TDAs) were established on the pattern of SFDA which addressed themselves to the problems of the tribal population. The level of investment in the new programme was much higher compared to TD Blocks. Six Tribal Development Agencies were started during the Fourth Plan and two more were added in the Fifth. Each Tribal Development agency covered a group of TD Blocks. They envisaged a more comprehensive frame than the SFDA which confined largely to agricultural and allied activities. The Tribal Development Agencies were expected to comprise elements of economic development, social services and prospective measures. In actual practice, however, the TDA became an agricultural development programme with added substantial investment in roads. This programme could not go beyond its pilot phase. The developmental effort in the tribal areas, therefore, continued largely in the form of TD Blocks. The early experience of TDAs and other programmes in rural areas provided a good base for the new phase of tribal development which began in the Fifth Plan.

Shilu Ao Committee

Review of the Tribal Development Programme was taken up by a study Team set-up by the Planning Commission under the chairmanship of Shilu Ao which submitted its report in 1969. The findings of this team had made it clear that it was necessary to adopt a flexible policy for tribal development. The main observation of this team regarding the Tribal Development Blocks was that although the achievement under the programme had generally fallen short of expectations, the programme had helped "to bring about a psychological change in the outlook of the tribals". Some of the main drawbacks pointed out by the Shilu Ao Team were:

(i) The Tribal Development Blocks failed to get any significant support from the general development programmes including the CD Programme;
(ii) The schemes formulated for these Blocks were not adopted to the felt needs of the specific areas;
(iii) The benefits had mostly accrued to the more advanced among the tribals; and
(iv) The TD Block was too small a geographical entity for coordinated planning. Programmes like education at secondary and higher levels, soil conservation and other programmes relating to infrastuctural development cut across block, district or even State boundaries and could not be financed out of the meagre allocation for the Tribal Development Blocks.

The team suggested that the programme for the tribal

development should be based on an "area approach" and should be financed out of the general plan supplemented in suitable cases by a special allocation for tribals.

The approach and strategy for tribal development was thus comprehensively reviewed on the eve of the Fifth Five Year Plan. As seen above the Shilu Ao Committee appointed by the Planning Commission during the Fourth Plan had already concluded that the TD Block, as it finally evolved, was an inadequate frame for tackling the complex problem of tribal development. It was already seen that the general rural development programmes were also struggling with the unresolved issues and many new experiments were on the anvil. In this context, a fresh look at the tribal scene gave a valuable insight and a new lead to the whole effort. It became clear that no single solution can be expected to have universal applicability to the entire tribal area since the situation in terms of resources, people, social constraints, infrastructural development and local priorities was entirely different in different regions. Yet, it was also appreciated that there was a common theme all through for which a broad frame would be necessary at the national level.

A Bipartite Division: A Two-way Classification

The entire question of tribal development has been broadly divided into two parts:

(a) areas of tribal concentrations; and
(b) dispersed tribal population.

The approach and strategy of tribal development in the two cases has to be quite distinct. The starting point of the new exercise was finding a satisfactory solution for the riddle of development in the national scene itself, viz. area development does not necessarily mean development of people living in that area. It was accepted that many an element of area development have to be incorporated in any plan even when it was designed as the people's development plan, particularly in the more backward regions. Infrastructural development acquires a special significance here. But the greatest caution has to be exercised constantly to ensure that infrastructure does not become an end in itself and is always kept at its proper place, viz. a means to the ultimate end of development of the community. Thus, infrastructural development properly adapted and as part of a bigger package may be a necessary condition but not a sufficient one for the people's development. Therefore, in those areas where the tribal population is predominant, investment on infrastructural development also becomes an element in tribal development. Thus a concept of "area development with focus on the development of tribal communities" has been evolved for the tribal areas.

Another important distinguishing feature of the areas of tribal concentration and dispersed tribals is the ownership of resources. A tribal community in the original state of economy has full command over the local resources. In the predominantly tribal areas, this ownership pattern has been disturbed, but only partially. On the other hand, in the case of dispersed tribals their command over resources is extremely limited. Therefore, there is a qualitative change in the initial conditions for tribal development in the two situations. It is easier to prevent deprivation and "running down" than to restore the original state once it has been disturbed.

The case of dispersed tribals is on a different footing. Infrastructural development in areas with dispersed tribals has to be a part of the general development programme. The focus of attention here has to be on the individual and the group. As we move to highly dispersed tribals, they tend to lose tribal characteristics and get assimilated in the mass of poor, particularly in the rural areas. They, however, continue to suffer from some additional social and, sometimes, economic limitations. The loss of command over resources and dispersal itself sometimes results in social regression.

The tribal communities generally have a very high social self-valuation as is evident from some of the names of tribal communities like "Ho"' which literally means "man". The tribal detached from his group and habitat is not able to adjust in a new surrounding. Resourceless, he cannot acquire a high social position. In many areas, he may even attract the stigma of untouchability as is the case with the Kotodis in Rajasthan, the Bhils in parts of western Madhya Pradesh and the Kols in the Bundelkhand region of Madhya Pradesh. The Kols are formally classified as Scheduled Castes in the neighbouring regions in Uttar Pradesh although they are just an extension of the larger tribal group living in Madhya Pradesh.

In the case of dispersed tribals, therefore, development has to be planned taking community or family as a unit. The approach cannot be that of area development even with the qualification of conscious focus on tribal development as has been accepted for the predominant tribal areas. In the case of dispersed tribals, we have to start with the man. Since he has no resource-base and majority of them are landless labourers, the emphasis in their case has to be on non-agricultural occupations.

Primitive Tribal Groups

Besides a broad two-way classification of tribals for the purposes of developmental strategy, some other special features are also notables. There are some tribal communities like the Onge, Bondo or Abujhmaria or Madia-Gonds who are caught at a nitch representing an earlier stage of economic development. They largely depend on food-gathering and hunting. Since the carrying capacity of local resources at the pre-agricultural level of technology is very limited, their population size is small. These communities are also generally pre-literate. Therefore, in the new strategy of development they have been treated as a separate group. In their case, a very flexible approach of development keeping in view the conditions of each specific group or the community has to be evolved. They have been termed as primitive tribal communities.

The Integrated Tribal Development Project (ITDP)

In pursuance of the above approach evolved on the eve of the Fifth Plan, a comprehensive programme of development was prepared, in the first stage, for areas of tribal concentration. The programme of primitive tribal communities was also given a high priority and specific schemes were drawn up for them. It was, however, decided that intensive development of dispersed tribal communities will be taken up in the second phase.

All areas with more than 50 per cent tribal population have been treated as predominantly tribal areas. Separate plans have been prepared for these areas, which are known as "Tribal Sub-Plans". In determining the population percentage of tribals in an area, the industrial and urban enclaves have been excluded. A tribal development block has been taken as the smallest unit for inclusion in the new programme. A group of blocks, which generally comprises a tehsil, has been taken as the basic unit for planning and development of the new tribal development programme. The unit is now known as Integrated Tribal Development Project (ITDP).

The degree of concentration of the tribal population in different States is significantly different. Therefore, the first delineation of the area of tribal concentration presented a very uneven situation. In some States such as Madhya Pradesh, Orissa and Bihar, it was possible to cover a substantial tribal population under the sub-Plans but in some others, this criterion did not yield an adequate coverage. The qualifying minimum size of the compact tribal majority area for inclusion in the Tribal Sub-Plans was reviewed with reference to the degree of tribal concentration obtaining in different States. A minimum population threshold of 20,000 was accepted as the smallest unit in Maharashtra, Andhra Pradesh and Assam. This norm was further relaxed to 10,000 in Tamil Nadu, Kerala and Uttar Pradesh. In the case of West Bengal and Tripura, it was necessary to go down still further and identify groups of villages for special development programmes. In Karnataka and Daman, it was not possible even to identify sizable villages of tribal concentration. The new programme in their case, therefore, was designed entirely for dispersed tribals.

In the quest for finding a viable population group for an effective and intensive developmental programme, it became necessary in some cases to have a second look at the existing administrative boundaries. It is noted earlier that the major tribal regions in the country are located in the border areas which comprise (i) southern Madhya Pradesh, southern Orissa, northern Andhra Pradesh and eastern Maharashtra, (ii) northern Orissa, southern Bihar, eastern Madhya Pradesh and western West Bengal, (iii) western Madhya Pradesh, southern Rajasthan, eastern Gujarat and north-western Maharashtra and (iv) Karnataka-Kerala-Tamil Nadu tri-junction.

The reason for this distribution is very simple. When the British extended their area of control from different centres in the country, outer boundaries of their influence were vaguely defined in the hilly and forest regions which were inaccessible as also difficult to subdue. Therefore, the tribal regions were the last to come under the effective control of the British power which finally determined the provincial and administrative boundaries. The result is that the otherwise compact tribal regions now fall within the jurisdiction of different States and are located in the inaccessible regions of all States. Similarly the compact tribal areas within a State are divided amongst a number of districts, taluks and blocks.

The delineation of the areas of tribal concentration was taken up in the beginning of the Fifth Plan and completed by the end of 1976. Although the Integrated Tribal Development Project was conceived as comprising a group of blocks, the actual size varied from State to State depending on the demographic structure of the tribal community in that region. The total number of Integrated Tribal Development Projects established by the beginning of 1978 was 180. An Integrated Tribal Development Project with more than One Block can be termed as a Meso Project and an ITDP comprising only one block or less than one block can be termed as Micro Project. Out of 180 ITDPs 121 are meso units and the remaining micro units. The sub-plans and ITDPs do not include the tribal majority states and Union Territories in whose case the plans of the States or the Union Territories, as the case may be, have been taken as plans for tribal development.

In their guidelines for the preparation of Sub-Plans and delineation of the Integrated Tribal Development Projects, the Planning Commission had desired that topography, local resources, demographic structure, social situation and level of development may be taken into consideration so that widely dissimilar areas are not included in the same project. Since an ITDP has been accepted as the unit of planning and implementation at the micro level, it was also desired that the administrative boundaries should not be changed unless considered essential. The average population size of the meso projects is 2.73 lakhs (1.62 lakh tribals) and the average geographical area is 3,265 sq. kms. The largest meso project in terms of population is Panchmahal in Gujarat with 10.24 lakhs (6.04 lakh Scheduled Tribes) population and the largest in terms of area is Spiti spread over 13,929 sq. kms. (Population 27,568 with 21,568 tribals).

The micro Projects themselves fall in two categories. Firstly, those micro projects in whose case the geographical area has been clearly delineated. The micro projects located in States having no substantial tribal concentration do not follow the general norm and do not represent the programme for an area. They comprise family-oriented or, at the best, hamlet-oriented programmes for tribal communities. They provide a preview exercise for programmes to be taken up in the second stage for dispersed tribals. The average population in area-specific micro projects is 43,000 (25,000 Scheduled Tribes) and the geographical area is 836 sq. kms. The smallest project in terms of population is Jalgaon in Maharashtra covering 9,000 people. The smallest in terms of area is Arunthumalai in Tamil Nadu spread over 29 sq. kms. The average scheduled tribe population of other non-area based micro projects is 58,000.

Based on the experience in the Fifth Plan, it was decided to extend the coverage of area-based tribal development programmes to pockets smaller than block units in all States. The Planning Commission agreed to include all pockets with 10,000 population and more than 50 per cent tribal concentration in the next phase of development.

The delineation of these areas progressed in various States. It covered a substantial tribal population under the Modified Area Development Approach (MADA) in Madhya Pradesh, Bihar, Orissa, Rajasthan, Gujarat and Maharashtra. A sizable population also got included in Andhra Pradesh. In other States, the norms for tribal sub-plans were already relaxed during the Fifth Plan. Therefore, this new extension of the Intensive Tribal Development Programme did not much increase the population coverage in these States.

According to the Constitution, the tribal communities are scheduled in specific areas for each State. After the reorganization of States in 1956 some anomalous position had arisen specially in the States of Madhya Pradesh, Maharashtra and Andhra Pradesh. A substantial part of tribal population in these States was recognized only in some districts. In 1976 this position was rationalized with the enforcement of the Constitution Order Scheduled Castes and Scheduled Tribes (Amendment) Act, 1976. All tribal communities are now recognized throughout the territory of a state unless specifically mentioned otherwise. This has increased the tribal population in the country by about 30.80 lakhs at 1971 base level. Since caste-wise figures are not collected in the Indian Census after 1941, it has not been possible to have accurate figures of newly added communities region-wise. Projections of additional population have been made on the 1931 figures and revised population figures have been adopted at the tehsil level. Some additional areas will be included in the intensive tribal development programmes based on these projections. A final picture, however, was available only after 1981 when all these communities could be enumerated afresh. About 80 per cent of the total tribals in the country were covered under intensive area development programmes taken up in the Sixth Plan.

Thus, intensive area-based programmes which are now extended to very small pockets (mini-MADA), will cover only about 80 per cent of the tribal population leaving 20 per cent outside their purview. The methodology for providing an intensive developmental coverage to the dispersed groups has been examined in details. It is accepted that it will be difficult to launch an effective programme exclusively for the dispersed tribals. The base of any such programme has to be the on-going general rural development scheme in that area. The various on-going rural development programmes had been reviewed and a common frame was provided under the Integrated Rural Development programme (IRD). Besides agricultural and allied sectors, rural industries have also been included in the IRD. It has also been decided that the unit of planning under the IRD will now be a block.

The members of the dispersed tribes in these areas have many common characteristics with rural poor but they may have some additional handicaps such as weakening social system, care-free nature, higher incidence of drinking, scanty political representation, etc. Therefore, the normal developmental programmes by themselves may not be adequate to solve their problems. It will therefore be necessary to pay special attention to the specific problems of the tribals in each Block. Although the Integrated Rural Development Programme had a wider frame and in particular included education, health and nutrition. Protective measures will also be taken in their case. Thus a comprehensive tribal development programme was formulated within the frame of the integrated rural development, to provide the additional inputs both organizational and physical wherever necessary.

Outlay for Tribal Development

The Constitution of India specifically provides for the financial needs of tribal areas. The ad-hoc provision, which used to be made in the early fifties under these obligatory provisions, was replaced by regular provision for development of the Scheduled Tribes distinctly under the Welfare of Backward Classes Sector both under the State and Central Plans. The provisions for the Scheduled Tribes are shown separately in this sector. These provisions are made under three broad categories, viz. (a) Education, (b) Economic Development, and (c) Health, Housing, etc. These provisions are designed as being supplemental to the investments in general programmes which cover the entire population and all areas.

Apart from the general outlays under the Welfare of Backward Classes, special outlays were also provided under various programmes taken up from time to time like Special Multipurpose Tribal Development Projects, Tribal Development Blocks and Tribal Development Agencies. The approach under these programmes was similar to that in the CD Blocks. It was envisaged that an intensive development effort would be made for each area. The programme would gradually pick up starting with an initial preparatory phase. After the intensive development activity for a period of five years, the programme would taper off with lesser investment. This was envisaged as a consolidation phase. It was expected that each Block area would, thus, reach the normal level of development in that region after which it would not require any additional investment. Thus, the TD Block was conceived in two stages of five years each with an investment of Rs. 10 lakhs in the first stage and Rs. 5 lakhs in the second stage. Since the review during the Fourth Plan showed that much remained to be done even after the second stage was complete, a third stage of five years was added with an investment of Rs. 10 lakhs.

The level of investment under the Tribal Development Agencies was of a much higher order. The Agency programme, however, did not cross the pilot stage when the new strategy for tribal development was adopted during the Fifth Plan.

The financial investments in the successive Five Year Plans have progressively increased. The outlays for tribal development have also been moving up as is shown in Tables 3.1 and 3.2.

TABLE 3.1: Growth of supplemental outlays for tribal development

(Rs. in crores)

Plan Period	Total Plan Size	State Sector	Central Sector	T.D.* Blocks	Total
First Plan	1,960	17.33	–	–	17.37
Second Plan	4,672	22.52	17.97	(4.03)	40.51
Third Plan	8,577	29.95	51.05	(15.53)	51.05
1966-69	6,756	10.46	24.86	(20.04)	35.32
Fourth Plan	16,160	37.70	46.50	(32.98)	84.20

* These figures are included in the figures of the Central Sector, hence given in brackets.

TABLE 3.2: Sector-wise supplemental outlays for tribal development

(Rs. in crores)

Plan Period	Education	Economic Uplift	Health Housing, etc.	Total
First Plan	5.10	8.46	3.81	17.37
Second Plan	8.05	22.70	9.76	40.51
Third Plan	13.23	30.72	7.10	51.05
1966-69	9.32	24.07	1.93	35.32
Fourth Plan	31.50	42.25	10.45	84.20

Total investment on tribal development has increased but as a proportion of total Plan outlay. It has not kept pace. The above figures, however, are only partial since they do not include the investments from the normal plan activity which accrued either to the tribal area as a part of area programme or the direct benefit to members of the tribal community as a part of target-oriented schemes. The total investment on tribal development is, therefore, substantially higher than indicated by these figures.

The Shilu Ao Committee, which was generally critical of the Tribal Development Block scheme, had also observed that the general programmes tended to bypass the tribal regions for a variety of reasons. Therefore, the investments which were expected to supplement the normal Plan effort in the tribal areas tended to supplant them. The TD Block programme bad become almost synonymous with tribal development. This situation, therefore, was corrected in the Fifth Plan with the preparation of sub-Plans.

The tribal sub-Plans represent the total development effort in the tribal region. They comprise four elements, viz.

(i) Investment for State Plans;
(ii) Investment for Central Plans;
(iii) Special Central Assistance for Tribal Development; and
(iv) Institutional Finance.

It was for the first time that the total investment for tribal development was brought under one frame which provided a check on the effort of individual departments and enabled the Planning Commission to consider adequacy or otherwise of the outlays. This approach has resulted in a substantial step-up in the financial investment. The outlays for tribal sub-Plans during the Fifth Plan (1974-79) was fixed at Rs. 1,440 crores out of which Rs. 975 crores were expected from State Plans, Rs. 78 crores from Central Ministries, Rs. 190 crores as Special Central Assistance and Rs. 197 crores as institutional finance. This approach has helped in the investments moving up substantially. The outlays in the first two years were small compared to the State Plan size. It is explained by the fact that the sub-Plans were in the process of formulation during that period. The investment picked up during the third year recording 75 per cent increase over the previous year and continued to grow at 33 per cent annum during the subsequent years and reached a reasonable proportion of State Plans during 1978-79.

Sector-wise Outlays

The sectoral breakup of the total outlay for the tribal development during the Fifth Plan shows that agricultural and allied sectors claimed the highest investment amounting to about 26 per cent followed be education and health services which accounted for about 21 per cent. Cooperation has been given a very high step-up during this Plan period with a total investment of Rs. 60 crores largely meant for marketing of agricultural and minor forest produces. Transport and communications had been kept at a low key claiming only about 8 per cent of the total investment. It has been possible to influence the pattern of investment from year to year as was seen from the approved outlays for 1978-79, the last year of the Fifth Plan. Out of a total investment of Rs. 405 crores, 121 crores or about 30 per cent of the total investment had gone for agriculture and allied sectors. Cooperation had claimed an outlay of Rs. 21 crores. Education and Health Services together claimed Rs. 88 crores or about 21 per cent of the total investment. The pattern of investment was thus, veering in favour of high priority programmes and schemes concerning the weaker sections of the community. A greater task of their adaptation and bringing about a qualitative change, however, remained to be performed.

The position of financial investment was reviewed (1977) by the Working Group on Tribal Development. The Group noted that the flow of investment from State Plans was satisfactory except in some States where much of their outlays was tied to area-specific or capital-intensive plans. The Working Group, however, noted that the investment from the Plans of the Central Ministries did not pick up. The Central Government had then decided to earmark outlays from Central Plans as well for the tribal areas. It was expected that the flow from financial institutions would also pick up as the project preparation gets a better technical base. The Working Group had estimated that the level of investment in tribal areas during 1978-83 would not be less than Rs. 3,000 crores comprising Rs. 1,850 crores from State Plans, Rs. 500 crores from Central Plans, Rs. 350 crores as Special Central assistance for tribal development and Rs. 300 crores from financial institutions.

Priorities in Programmes

The concept of tribal development was kept comprehensive from the very beginning. It covers all aspects of the social and economic life of the tribal communities. However, when the programmes under TD Blocks were prepared their ambit, in operational terms, was very limited. They concerned themselves largely with the usual developmental schemes and social services. These schemes were generally formulated for the comparatively advanced areas and extended to the tribal areas in the same form. The protective aspects were emphasized in principle but they were not organically linked with other facets of administration and development. In the Fifth Plan full stock of the tribal situation was taken and an attempt made to spell out a clear operational strategy.

It was realized that the very process of development was making the tribal communities more vulnerable. The total impact was not only not neutral but adverse to the tribal interest. Protective measures in the immediate context, with the clear objective of elimination of exploitation in all forms, had to be assigned the highest priority. The various policies of the Government and practices in vogue in the area were reviewed. Protective measures, however, could be only ad-interm in nature. Consequently, steps needed to be taken concurrently for building up the inner strength of the community to enable them to partake in the benefits accruing to the area as a result of general developmental programmes and to face the new competitive situations, which were emerging in these areas, with confidence and on terms of equality. Education and social services, therefore, had been assigned the next highest priority in the new programme. Economic development programme per se, thus, came to occupy a much lower position than what would have been the case otherwise. In the economic programmes those having direct relevance to the average tribal, particularly the weakest groups, had been given a higher priority compared to the bigger programmes. Building of infrastructure as an independent item of development got relegated to the background unless a scheme was directly linked to an economic activity of higher priority.

While the broad strategy, as outlined above, was applicable to the tribal region as a whole, the details had to be worked out for each area depending on the local socio-economic situation. A specific programme was, therefore, prepared for each Integrated Tribal Development Project. Even a project may have considerable variation within its own boundary in terms of topography, resource potential, demographic characteristics and the intensity of on-going economic activity. Therefore, a balance had to be worked out even within a project and it had to be ensured that the regional disparities are reduced and the problem of the weakest groups continues to get the highest priority.

It may be noted here that although the approach and strategy have been clearly worked out, the success so far, both in detailed planning and implementation of programmes had been rather limited if viewed in terms of these priorities. The bigger programmes continue to dominate the scene because of operational convenience and more articulate groups being interested in them. Similarly infrastructural development has been continually pressed on the ground that it is the first necessary step for people's development. The Working Group on Tribal Development, which reviewed the position, observed that elimination of exploitation had only limited success. There had been sepectacular success in relation to the level of investment in these areas which have grown phenomenally in the last four years. But even here the bigger programmes and infrastructural development have stolen the march, while small programmes of direct relevance to the tribals have not substantially picked up. Administrative unpreparedness appears to have come up as an important constraint in the effective implementation of tribal development programmes and protective policies.

These aberrations were corrected in the medium-term Plan (1978-83) for tribal development. Administration of tribal areas and implementation arrangements were specially reviewed. The Working

Group on Tribal Development made a number of important recommendations which were accepted by the Government of India. A greater use of the provisions in the Fifth Schedule was visualized to simplify the administrative system and to cut the procedural lags. These provisions may also be used for establishing a clear chain of command with specific responsibility and built-in accountability.

The priorities in developmental programmes broadly follow the approach adopted in the Fifth Plan. However, education had now been accepted as the highest priority programme per se and all necessary investments will be made available for the universalization of elementary education, improving its quality and eradication of illiteracy, according to a clear time schedule. The relationship between the administration and the community was also to undergo a structural change. It was accepted that the Village Panchayat should oversee all developmental programmes in the tribal areas. They were also to be enabled to attend to all aspects of citizens' problem in their dealings with the administration. The extension agency was to be redesigned with building up a member of the local community in each village as a diffusion point who would be a part of the system though formally outside it.

A Turning Point : The Fifth Five Year Plan

On the eve of the Fifth Plan, the Planning Commission set-up a Task Force in 1971 which reviewed the tribal situation comprehensively and recommended a perspective for the development of tribal areas in the country. These were kept in view while formulating the policy, approach and strategy for the Fifth Five Year Plan. The problem of tribal development basically pertained to the development of three categories of tribals:

(a) Areas of tribal concentration;
(b) Dispersed tribals; and
(c) Primitive tribal communities.

While evolving the strategy for the Fifth Plan, it was felt that attention had to be focused on the specific problem of each identifiable group and area. The situations in regions of tribal concentration and in areas of dispersed tribal population would be quite distinct and would require different approaches. In the regions of tribal concentration, area development approach had to be adopted, keeping the focus on the problems of the tribal people. In the case of dispersed tribal population, family approach would have to be adopted. It was also felt that category (c) which included certain very backward and isolated smaller groups faced problems of their very survival and would have to be treated as a special category, both within the areas of tribal concentration and outside, and special group-oriented programmes would have to be formulated for them.

The basic approach towards tribal development adopted in the Fifth Plan was to identify larger areas of tribal concentration which included the Scheduled Areas, contiguous TD Blocks and other blocks/areas having 50 per cent tribal concentration. All such blocks/areas in a State were to be brought under a separate sub-Plan under the overall State Plan. However, States and Union Territories which have predominant tribal population like Nagaland, Meghalaya, Arunachal Pradesh, Mizoram and Lakshadweep were not required to draw up separate sub-Plans, because the entire State Plan in these cases was basically for the welfare of the tribals.

For the preparation of the tribal sub-Plans, the Planning Commission issued a set of guidelines to the States. The guidelines spelt out the long-term objective of the tribal sub-Plan as (1) Narrowing the gap between the levels of development of tribals and other areas, and (2) Improving their quality of life. Among the immediate objectives were (1) Elimination of exploitation in all forms, (2) Speeding up of the processes for social and economic development, (3) Building up the inner strength of the people, and (4) Improving their organizational capabilities. The guidelines laid down the criteria for identification of the sub-Plan areas, the approach and strategy for their development and also the pattern of funding and formulation of programmes in these areas. The guidelines also stated that the sub-Plan areas in each State should comprise a number of viable projects. For each such Integrated Tribal Development Project (ITDP) an integrated area development plan focussing attention on the specific problems of the area and the tribal people was to be formulated. The sub-Plan areas in each State thus comprised a number of viable projects.

Identification and Demarcation of Sub-Plan Areas

In addition to the scheduled areas, each State identified the

Tehsils/Talukas/Blocks having a tribal concentration of 50 per cent or more. From these, suitable planning areas were carved out at macro- meso- and micro-levels, keeping in view the natural resources, physical features, level of development of the tribes inhabiting the region and other socio-economic considerations to suit the planning functions at these levels. It was laid down that these areas should, to the extent possible, conform to the existing administrative boundaries. For instance, macro areas were constituted in a manner in which they conveniently fell into separate revenue divisions/districts. Similarly, micro areas normally coincided with CD/TD Blocks. As a general rule, a TD/CD Block was taken as the lowest unit except in States which have a large dispersed tribal population. Between the macro and micro areas was the meso area, popularly called the "project area" (ITDP), which was formed by grouping of contiguous Development Blocks and is generally coterminous with a Taluka/Tehsil/Sub-Division and in some cases District also. In the case of Madhya Pradesh, Orissa and Bihar, more than one district tribal region spread over a number of districts formed sub-Plan areas. These States have, thus, more than one macro region for tribal development. By the end of the Fifth Plan 179 projects (ITDPs) had been identified in the entire tribal sub-Plan area in the country.

The planning function at the macro/meso level, depending on local conditions, included overall planning and detailed project formulation for rural electrification, major and medium irrigation projects, arterial roads, apex cooperative organizations, processing industries, etc. At the micro level, which is the Block level, planning for social services, minimum needs programme, minor irrigation, agricultural extension and household industries were to be undertaken.

Evolution of the Concept of Tribal Sub-Plan

The Fifth Plan period will be remembered more for the birth and evolution of the concept of sub-Plan for the tribal regions of State within the overall frame of the State Plan. The objective of the tribal sub-Plan has been spelt as development of the area with focus on the scheduled Tribe population within the sub-Plan area. Briefly, the concept consists identification of Development Blocks within a State having more than 50 per cent Scheduled Tribe population and launching of a massive effort for tribal development within that "sub-Plan Area". The effort has been conceived as total in the financial and physical senses. This means that the totality of financial resources available is required to be channelized as investment in the tribal areas and a total matching physical effort is to be mounted to translate the investment into concrete benefits for the tribal families. The unit of planning, an Integrated Tribal Development Project (ITDP) in a State, comprised an aggregate of development Blocks. The ITDP being smaller than a district and bigger than a Development Block appears more feasible for planning. The lowest unit of execution of the programme is the Development Block; it has a development team with the Block Development Officer as its leader. Programmes have to be planned for an ITDP in the shape of a sub-Plan for the tribal region of the State. Guidelines laid down that planning should be based on the needs of the area and the people, and hence, the process has to be commenced at the grass-root level, i.e. the Development Block, and funnelled upwards to the ITDP, State and national levels.

The idea of totality needs some elaboration. Taking the financial aspect first, in a State the chief financial source of development is the State Plan funds of the Centrally sponsored schemes and Central schemes being an addition thereto. In the tribal sub-Plan areas, these funds are supplemented by special Central assistance provided by the Centre in pursuance of the constitutional provision making tribal development the special responsibility of the Union Government. For family-oriented schemes, while the subsidy component is drawn from Government funds, the loan component is provided by financial institutions, thus making the latter a very important source. This pool of funds has to be used for undertaking a synergistic package of schemes in a Development Block, keeping in view the natural resource endowment and the needs of the people. It is the intention that the Five Year Project Report and the Annual Plans of an ITDP should reflect the socio-economic aspirations in the ITDP, the total quantum of resources available and the means to be adopted for achieving the objective. Area planning approach has been adopted as the tribal sub-Plan areas have poor infrastructure and contain non-tribal population in addition to the tribal population. About 65 per cent of the total Scheduled Tribe population in the country was covered in the Fifth Plan period.

Strategy in the Fifth Plan

A general strategy was evolved by each State for the development of its tribal areas keeping in view the special problems of the tribal regions, in consultation with the Planning Commission and the Ministry of Home Affairs of the Government of India. The entire legal and institutional frame, the inter and intra-sectoral priorities were reviewed keeping welfare and development of the Scheduled Tribes as the primary focus in the Plan programme of the area. Some of the main points of the strategy in the Fifth Five Year Plan were:

Prevention of Exploitation

It was realized that no developmental activity could be of benefit to the tribal population unless their exploitation was prevented and integrated credit-cum-marketing services developed in the sub-Plan areas. These services covered marketing of agricultural and minor forest produce, supply of inputs and essential consumer commodities. Credit for productive, consumption and social needs was made available to the tribals in the sub-Plan areas. The credit and marketing structure in these areas was reorganized into Large Agricultural Multi-purpose Societies (LAMPS) in accordance with the recommendations of the Bawa Committee set-up by the Ministry of Agriculture, Government of India, to study the problem. Efforts were made for the past debt redemption of the tribals through legislative and executive measures. Programme for prevention of land alienation, restoration of land already alienated and rehabilitation of bonded labour were taken up. Attention was also given to the solution of problems created among the tribal society on account of modern industries being developed in these areas. The Excise and Forest policies which directly affected tribals were also reviewed to protect the interests of these people.

Development of Tribal Agriculture

High priority was given to tribal agriculture. The most important aspects of tribal agriculture development are ownership rights, completion of land records, land development and introduction of improved methods of agriculture through extension services. Special attention was given to shifting cultivators, forest villages and forest labourers through schemes of plantation, afforestation, Forest Labour Cooperative Societies, etc.

Generation of Employment Opportunities

Employment opportunities for better utilization of available manpower were created through programmes which could be easily inducted into tribal economy like horticulture, animal husbandry, poultry, piggery, etc., and cottage industries based on local raw materials.

Provision of Basic Infrastructure

In order to accelerate socio-economic development, special attention was given to the creation of basic infrastructure, legal, institutional and physical, growth centres, communication network, schools, health centres, marketing and credit organization, rural electrification, manpower resources and training facilities were required to be planned in an integrated fashion keeping in view the special conditions of the tribal areas.

Special Groups and their Problems

Even within the tribal areas, the primitive tribal groups, extremely backward pockets, shifting cultivators and tribals affected by major industrial projects were given special attention by drawing up different schemes which would help these groups.

Each sectoral authority was required to review sectoral programmes beings implemented in the sub-Plan areas in order to adapt them to the special needs of these areas. The programmes in these areas were categorized as Core Programmes and Other Programmes. The Core Programmes included credit and marketing, preparation of land records, restoration of alienated land, crop husbandry, training of farmers, minor and medium irrigation, forest-based programmes, special problems, primary road network linking important market and growth centres, rationalization of administrative structure and techno-economic survey and evaluation studies.

Funding Strategy for the Sub-Plan

The resources available for the tribal sub Plan comprised:

(a) State plan outlays;
(b) Sectoral outlays in the Central Ministries for the tribal sub-Plan areas;
(c) Special central assistance for the tribal sub-Plan areas; and
(d) Institutional finance.

The basic frame for the development of these areas was provided by the State Plan. The flow of funds from the State Plan for the Tribal Sub-Plan was worked out on the basis of total population of the sub-Plan area, its geographical area, its comparative level of development and of social services. The actual share of the Tribal sub-Plan out of the State Plan was quantified out of the divisible pool of the State Plan resources with a weightage for the backwardness of the sub-Plan area. The investment of the non-divisible pool such as power, major irrigation and industrial projects were generally in accordance with the actual benefits accruing to these regions. A special Central assistance meant to augment the efforts of the State was added to the State Plans on the basis of an accepted formula. The Central Ministries were also required to identify Central and Centrally sponsored schemes which would benefit the tribal areas.

Another important feature regarding the outlays for tribal development was that funds should be made non-divertible. So far as the Special Central Assistance is concerned, it is already a charge on the Consolidated Fund of India and has a special status. The first step towards non-divertibility of the State Plan outlay has been to introduce separate budget sub-heads under each major head of development. This was an important step for systematizing and consolidating the developmental efforts in the tribal sub-Plan areas and bringing some accountability. In some States like Madhya Pradesh, the entire sub-Plan outlay for tribal development has been brought under one single demand. The Secretary, Tribal Welfare Department, or the Tribal Development Commissioner has been nominated as the Chief Controlling Officer for this single demand. This has helped in greater flexibility in inter-sectoral reallocations and ensuring non-divertibility. A workable mechanism in those States where the sectoral sub-Plan outlays continue to be budgeted under the separate demands is gradually being evolved to ensure non-divertibility, flexibility and accountability.

Administrative Structure

The tribal areas were, till Independence, administered only minimally, where only forest guards and occasionally police were in charge of some sort of administration. Obviously the needs of the tribal people were neglected. Their exploitation by the middlemen, excise and forestry personnel impoverished the tribal society. After Independence and with the development programmes being implemented, a multiplicity of administrative agencies came into existence. When TD Blocks were set-up, the right type of development personnel were not forthcoming for lack of incentive to work in remote areas, as well as lack of understanding of the problems of the tribal people amongst whom they were required to work. Therefore, a suitable administrative set-up was devised by each State for the sub-Plan area depending upon the particular requirements of the area and the existing infrastructure. Multiplicity of agencies was to be avoided in the tribal areas as it led to diffusion of responsibility, inadequate control and lack of coordination. Efforts were therefore, made to build into the system adequate flexibility along with specificity of responsibility and individual authority.

Fifth Plan Efforts

By the end of the Fifth Plan, 18 States and Union Territories had drawn up Tribal Sub-Plans covering 65 per cent of the tribal population in the country. The entire Tribal Sub-Plan area in the country had been divided into 179 projects (ITDPs). Although the sub-Plan strategy was new and the sub-Plan started taking a concrete shape only in 1975-76, even then by the end of the Fifth Plan period project reports had been prepared for 129 out of the 179 projects.

In terms of financial investment, the State Governments had quantified Rs. 601 crores as outlays from general sectors of development and the special central assistance for the sub-Plan amounted to Rs. 120 crores. Investments from Central Ministries Plans could not, however, be clearly indentified. As will appear from Table 3.3, the percentage of flow of funds from the State Plans has been steadily going up from year to year and from the Fifth Plan to the Sixth Plan.

The preparation of Annual Sub-Plans became a concurrent exercise with the State Annual Plans. Thereafter, the annual Sub-Plans so prepared were disaggregated project-wise. The ideal situation would have been that the sub-Plans were prepared from the project level upward. This could not, however, be done in most of the States. In the early stages of a new strategy, some divergence between the normative frame and the actual programme profile is inevitable for some time. However, it has been possible for the States to narrow this gap with the successive Annual Plans and greater association of the project authorities with the planning process.

TABLE 3.3: Percentage flow of funds from State Plans to State Sub-Plans (1974-75 – 1979-80)

(Rs. in crores)

	Total State Plan	Total State Sub-Plan	Percentage of Sub-Plan to Total Plan	Special Central Assistance
1974-75	1844	43*	–	5.00
1975-76	2660	109	4.10	20.00
1976-77	3215	192	5.96	40.00
1977-78	3874	257	6.64	55.00
1978-79	4975	344	6.92	70.00
1979-80	4987	394	7.90	70.00

*Rough estimates made on the basis of the programmes implemented.

The sub-Plan strategy lays emphasis on administrative structure and proper personnel policy. The concept that tribal development is the responsibility of all development departments has now been reasonably settled. At the ITDP level, the collective responsibility of different departments has also been accepted. Almost all State have appointed or agreed to appoint senior officers as project officers. The Project Authority, comprising various Heads of Departments, the Collector and the Project Officer have been charged with the responsibility to implement the total development programme. However, the integration of all sectoral programmes at the project level has still to be fully achieved.

The first sub-Plan spelt out the broad strategy and priorities in different States. A broad consensus was arrived at regarding the various issues affecting the tribal population. Elimination of exploitation was given the highest priority. It was agreed that the problem of land alienation needs to be tackled as a time-bound programme. Priority was also to be given to marketing and credit to do away with the middlemen and the money lender, and with this view 2,216 Large Agricultural Multi-purpose Societies (LAMPS) were organized.

A review done by the Working Group on Tribal Development constituted for the preparation of the Sixth Plan revealed that although the approach and priorities in the programme had been clearly worked out, the programmes had not yet picked up. Elimination of exploitation had limited success. Although these had been a spectacular success in relation to the level of investments in these Tribal Sub-Plan areas, programmes of infrastructural development such as roads, electricity, buildings, etc., dominated over smaller programmes of direct benefit to the tribal families. The working Group observed that administrative preparedness had come up "as an important constraint in the effective implementation of tribal development programmes and protective policies".

The Fifth Plan had also envisaged special programmes to be taken up by State Governments for the primitive tribal groups at pre-agricultural levels of technology, or who had remained extremely backward due to social and economic reasons. Though not much headway could be made in this direction, a total number of 52 communities or groups had been identified for whom the project reports were required to be prepared.

Sixth Plan-Extension of Sub-Plan Approach

The experience of planning in areas of tribal concentration indicated that the broad approach to tribal development will have to depend on the pattern of distribution of tribals in an area and the level of their economy. In areas of tribal concentration, an area approach with the focus on tribal communities will have to be continued as in the Fifth Plan; the dispersed population would be covered by family-oriented programmes and community-oriented special programmes will have to be evolved and implemented for primitive groups. Since a CD/TD block was adopted as the smallest unit for inclusion in the tribal sub-Plan, substantial portion of dispersed tribal population could not get the benefits of the area approach. The

Draft Sixth Plan, therefore, provided for extension of sub-Plan approach to additional areas of 10,000 population with a tribal concentration of 50 per cent and above. It was estimated that an additional 10 per cent of the country's tribal population would be covered by the extension of the sub-Plan strategy.

The long-term objectives in the Sixth Plan continued to be the same as in the Fifth Plan, viz.

(i) narrowing the gap between the level of development of tribal areas and others; and
(ii) improving the quality of life of the tribal people.

The strategy of development lays emphasis on consolidation of the gains of protective measures, programmes of full employment, education and health services. The programmes under different sectors of development are required to be intensified with suitable modifications to remove the present inadequacies in implementation.

The States have to give due importance to the integration of programmes in the field and effective delegation of powers to the Project Authorities in ITDPs. Since implementation of a programme depends largely on the quality of personnel, some institutional arrangement has to be made by States for posting of suitable officers in these areas who can work with devotion and understanding. Orientation training of personnel has to be given special attention.

The approach in the Sixth Plan 1978-83 for the development of backward areas in general was to rely, to a greater extent, on the development of agriculture, village and small-scale industries, subsidiary occupations and related services and also the Minimum Need Programmes and Area Development Programmes. As the tribal regions fall in different agro-climatic regions, a clear strategy for agricultural development of each region has to be worked out. Adaptive research, large-scale field trials of proved techniques and identification of major-thrust areas have been considered essential. Improvement of economic status of the tribals should be the first concern and suitable programmes of horticulture, cattle development, poultry and piggery, etc., should be taken up. Shifting cultivators have to get due attention which they have failed to get so far. The forest policy in its various aspects affecting the tribal needs to be implemented. In respect of these economic programmes, the role of the marketing and credit organizations such as LAMPS has been re-emphasized. This would help to eliminate the middleman and the money-lender and thereby give economic benefits direct to tribal population. The economy of tribal artisans is getting adversely affected on account of a competitive market. Promotion of tribal crafts and family-based programmes for helping these groups including marketing facilities have to be formulated. Integrated development of tribal communities under the zones of influence of the industrial projects requires to be taken up. Some areas like the hinterland of industrial and mining complexes, forest-rich regions and areas with a high landless population will need special attention and for them separate Plans will have to be prepared. These regions should be indentified and special provisions made for them in the sub-Plans.

After the Fifth Plan the planning process received a set-back due to a change in the government at the Centre. The Janata Party came to power and formulated its Sixth Plan for 1978-83 which laid stress on the Minimum Needs Programmes.

After the defeat of the Party the Congress party came to power and introduced a new Sixth Plan (1980-81 to 1984-85) which took into account the short-coming of the previous plan. The total size of the tribal Sub-Plan during the period was estimated to be of Rs. 5,000 crores. The outlay and expenditure on the socio-economic programmes for the scheduled Tribes during the Sixth Plan has been shown in Table 3.4.

TABLE 3.4: Sixth Plan outlays on socio-economic programmes for the Scheduled Tribes

(Rs. in crores)

S.No.	Fund From	Sixth Plan Outlays	Sixth Plan Expenditure
(1)	States' allocation for Tribal Sub-Plan	3521	3409
(2)	Special Central Assistance*	485	485
(3)	Institutional Finance	NA	800

* Funds from Special Component Plan to ensure a higher degree of devolution of funds.

During the Sixth Plan, Sikkim was added to the States covered under the Tribal Sub-Plan. There were now 180 ITDPs, and the coverage of tribal population was raised to 75 per cent, while the number of primitive tribes identified was raised from 52 to 75.

Emphasis was placed more on family-oriented programmes than on infrastructure development unlike in the previous Plans. Special Component Plans (SCPs) had a Special Central Assistance Counterpart by way of addition to the States Plan Programme. It was proposed to assist 50 per cent of the Scheduled Tribes families to cross over the poverty line and as against a target of 2.70 million S.T. families to be brought above the poverty line 3.46 million S.T. families received this assistance though it was not certain whether they had actually crossed the poverty line or required further assistance.

About 9,000 villages were electrified and 80,000 provided with supply of drinking water.

Seventh Plan – TSP Benefits Extended to all Tribals

The Seventh Five Year Plan (1985-90) with a huge public sector outlay of Rs. 154,220 crores was quite ambitious though it became difficult to mobilize the amount. The programme of tribal development with ITDP pattern was continued without any basic or major changes in the approach, pattern or structure, but better coordination was sought between various agencies, and social services were given priority. It was admitted that the planning process in the tribal areas had to be a judicious mixture of beneficiary-oriented programmes, human resource development and infrastructure development and during the Seventh Plan, the first 30 lakh tribal families in the TSP were to be assisted to build up their economic base. Socio-economic development of the tribal areas as well as of the tribal families was to continue.

LAMPS (Large Agricultural Marketing Societies) in tribal areas were to be strengthened through broadening their popular base. Plan formulation and project reports were to be made in close consultation with the beneficiaries. Scientific project reports were to be prepared for ITDD and primitive tribal groups. The Special Central Assistance for the TSP was fixed at Rs. 756 crores in the Seventh Plan. Rehabilitation stress on the removal of tribal women's backwardness were envisaged. Care was also to be taken to see that development did not directly or indirectly clash with the customary modes and usages of the tribal areas.

It shows that the objectives of the strategy during all the Plans (up to the Seventh Plan) remained two-fold:

(i) Socio-economic development of the scheduled Tribes; and
(ii) Protection of tribals against exploitation.

For the implementation, the Integrated Tribal Development Projects (ITDPs) were conceived during the Fifth Five Year Plan: and have since been continued. During the Sixth Plan, Modified Area Development Approach (MADA) was adopted to cover smaller areas of tribal concentration having 10,000 or more population of which 50 per cent or more are tribals. During the Seventh Plan, Clusters of tribal concentration with 5,000 or more population with 50 per cent or more tribal population were identified.

During the Seventh Plan period, the Tribal Sub-Plan strategy benefits were extended to all the tribals including the dispersed tribals who were not covered by the ITDPs, MADA, cluster groups and primitive groups. Family-oriented programmes were extended to them. By the end of the Seventh Plan the Position was as under:

		S.T. Population Covered
ITDPs	191	303.41 lakhs
MADAs	268	45.82 lakhs
Cluster areas	74	3.43 lakhs

All these are in 19 TSP States and Union Territories.

In all, 75 primitive tribal groups were identified in 15 States/Union Territories covering 16.36 lakh Scheduled Tribes population which are characterized by :

(i) low rate of growth of population,
(ii) pre-agricultural level of technology, and
(iii) low level of literacy.

The total expenditure for the development of Scheduled Tribes from the Fifth to the Seventh Plan period in shown in table 3.5.

TABLE 3.5 Expenditure in different Plan periods for development of Scheduled Tribes

(Rs. in crores)

	Funds From		
	State Plan	Special Central Assistance	Total
Fifth plan	759.44	186.76	946.20
1979-80 (Actual)	382.45	59.45	441.90
Sixth Plan	3387.89	486.11	3874.00
Seventh Plan (1985-90) (Provisional)	7100.57	851.25	7951.82

Source: A Note on Review of Programmes during the Seventh Plan, Planning Commission, New Delhi, p. 2.)

Eighth Plan—Approach Paper

The Eighth Five Year Plan which was started late, i.e. from 1992, in the Approach Paper (1990-95) takes note of the following:*

(1) The resource base and the socio-cultural heritage of our Scheduled Tribe population is getting eroded through a combination of development interventions, commercial exploitation and ineffective legal and administrative system.

(2) Projects for irrigation, power transport, etc., often disrupt the life and environment of a large number of Scheduled Tribe families, while the benefits accrue mainly to population on the plains. Measures for relief and rehabilitation in such cases have been neither imaginatively conceived nor whole-heartedly need to be shown to this dimension.

(3) Programmes need to be devised with the involvement of the Scheduled Tribes themselves in the light of their own order of priorities to remove economic, educational and social disparities. The line of action should include, besides access to minimum social services, assistance in scientific resource conservation, construction of small water-harvesting and storage systems, restoration of their traditional rights in the

* *G.O.I. Approach to the Eighth Five Year Plan*, Planning Commission, New Delhi, May, 1990, pp. 31-32.

forest produce and direct links with market and strengthening of their traditional community organizations.

Objectives During the Eighth Plan

The main objectives of tribal development envisaged during the Eighth Plan were:

(a) Effective tackling of exploitative practices in tribal areas in matters related to alienation of land, right to collection of forest produce, payment of proper wages for their labour, remunerative prices for their produce to ensure sustained flow and full utilization of benefits of the Plan programme;
(b) Ensure full rehabilitation of displaced tribals due to establishment of projects;
(c) Emphasis on development of essential infrastructure facilities to achieve the objective of assisting the targeted number of tribal families to cross the poverty line and increasing their access to health, education and employment opportunities;
(d) Full implementation of projects for integrated development of identified primitive tribal groups;
(e) Special focus on programmes to deal with the education and health needs of tribal women;
(f) Restructuring and defining the TSP strategy to ensure adequate qualification for TSP adoption of schemes to suit the needs of the tribal people, adequate per tribal family assistance and participation of tribal beneficiaries;
(g) Emphasis on monitoring and evaluation of programmes;
(h) There are some Tribal Sub-Plan districts in the country which have more than 50 per cent Scheduled Tribes and which are also specified as Scheduled Areas under the Fifth Schedule to the Constitution. In these districts, relevant area-based and family-oriented schemes on need-based criteria, backed by an effective administrative set-up supported by provisions under the Fifth Schedule to the Constitution, were to be effectively taken up. It was felt that such an innovation in the TSP approach might yield better results.

As an experimental measure, the full districts numbering about 26 in different States under the TSP were to be brought under a unified administrative structure (DRDAs and ITDPs) and all financial and administrative powers for the socio-economic development of tribals were to be vested in an officer of the rank of District Collector.

Involvement of traditional tribal institutions in planning, implementing and monitoring of programmes should be ensured.

Socio-Economic Groups for Scheduled Castes and Tribes

The Planning Commission appointed Socio-Economic Groups for the Scheduled Castes and the Scheduled Tribes (separately) for formulation of schemes for the Eighth Five Year Plan. These groups were created by the Backward Classes Division of the Planning Commission. After deliberations and discussions the groups made recommendations. The main recommendations and suggestions made by the Group on the Scheduled Tribes are given below.

Main Recommendations/Suggestions

Development of Scheduled Tribes

(1) The Central Advisory Council for Harijans and Schedule Tribes which were in existence till about April, 1960 should be revived.
(2) The single line administration is undemocratic and the self-managment provisions available under the Sixth Schedule should be made applicable to Fifth Schedule Areas.
(3) The norms for setting up adult education centres were too unrealistic and did not take into account the various socio-economic groups within the area of the Centres i.e. SCs and STs, low level of literacy etc. of certain groups. The norms should be revised.
(4) Universities should be involved in a more effective manner in the programmes of Ministry of Welfare, to train SC/ST candidates to compete successfully in the entry-examinations for public services.
(5) The earlier scheme of assisting forest villages under grants-in-aid to proviso (1) of Article 275 of the Constitution should be revived.
(6) The report of the Committee on Programmes under Poverty

Alleviation (MHA) should be implemented.

(7) Special attention should be paid to small primitive tribal groups numbering 74.

(8) There was enough scope to improve the economy of tribal people through collection, processing and marketing of minor forest produce and in particular medicinal plants.

(9) Centrally Sponsored Schemes meant for scheduled tribes should not be transferred to the States.

(10) Integrated system of health services and use of mobile dispensaries should be promoted in tribal areas.

(11) Drop-outs at primary level was a serious problem and remedial measures should be taken.

(12) There was need for unified administrative structure in tribal areas.

(13) Traditional tribal institutions and their community spirit should be used for tackling developmental problems of tribal areas and managing their own affairs.

(14) All-weather roads in tribal areas is a necessity.

(15) Employment programmes should be linked with local resources.

(16) Exploitation should be tackled on a priority basis.

(17) Voluntary and social service organisations of non-political character should be involved in promoting developmental activities.

(18) Consumption of liquor by personnel serving in tribal areas should be prohibited.

(19) Endeavour should be made to wean tribals away from drinking.

(20) Single line administration provided accountability and commitment.

(21) Land is a basic resource of tribals.

(22) The working of Scheduled Castes and Scheduled Tribes development Corporations need toning up.

(23) Right to life should be protected which meant command over resources.

(24) The autonomy of tribal villages should be ensured and the district and village councils will have to play an important role.

(25) Minor Forest Produce Prices Commission be set up.

(26) Educational development should be accorded highest priority.

(27) Autonomous district councils may not be as effective as autonomous village councils.

(28) Country liquor shops in tribal areas should be closed down.

(29) Panchayti Raj system will not work for the benefit of Schedule Castes and Scheduled Tribes unless these bodies are wholly composed of SCs/STs.

4

TRIBAL SUB-PLAN : A Special Strategy

THE Tribal populations are extremely poor and backward. Though the planning process was initiated in 1951-52, the rate of economic development of all the weaker sections of the community and particularly the tribals had been extremely low in spite of special programmes for them.

The hilly inaccessible areas generally unconnected by road have been the abode of the tirbals for centuries and are primarily responsible for isolating them from the main stream of Indian populace. This isolation has further led to lack of education, inadequate means of livelihood, abyssmal ignorance, etc., resulting in their inhuman exploitation. In quite a few instances their social customs and taboos have proved a hindrance to their assimilation of even primary economic techniques and facilities. The action and interaction of the above mentioned factors are the main causes for their deprival of the planned development benefits.

The restructuring of the Indian society on socialist lines needs accelerating of the tempo of economic development of society and especially of the weaker sections. However, this aim could be achieved only if there is a total reorientation in the existing planning process and the planning machinery set-up to tackle the developmental problems of the general population as the same will prove to be totally inadequate for the purpose at hand. The Government's decision to break new ground in this matter was the measure of its realization of the state of affairas and chalking out of a 15-year perspective Plan beginning from the Fifth Plan for tribal development reflected its sense of realism and urgency as one Plan period or two would have proved inadequate for the same.

For concretizing the aims and perspective set before itself in respect of the tribals the Government decided to weild the instrument of a sub-Plan within the State's Fifth Plan. The urgency of reaching the goal and the dire necessity of obtaining results in the matter of tribal development led to the rearrangement of Plan priorities and setting up of a powerful State-lavel Steering Committee chaired by the State's Finance Minister to chalk out the modalities and details of the sub-Plan. This also indicated that economic development of the weaker sections like tribals received top priority at the hands of the Government. This Committee after touring the tribal areas, meeting the *Adivasis* and their leadership, acquainting itself with their problems and felt needs, and analysing in depth the causes of their backwardness and other cognate issues drew up a blue print for progress and allround development of the tribals. Stopping of exploitation at the hands of unscrupulous money-lenders and rapacious traders, provision of basic low-level economic facilities to enable an *Adivasi* to increase his productive capacity and consequential increase in his economic ability to absorb higher techniques of productive processes, breaking of the communication barrier between him and the general populace so that he forms part of society's mainstream by road-building programmes, expanding his horizon of assimilation capacity by introducing educational facilities were the main pillars on which the sub-Plan edifice was made to rest in the blue print for progress.

The operational success of any programme for development is directly dependent upon the people's active participation from the drawing board through to the implementation stage of any scheme. The State's switch-over to the concept of district planning was a step in the right direction of people's participation and it assured that the Plan blueprints which thus emerged reflected the people's felt needs and problems and answer for the same. As a matter of fact the sub-Plan blueprint was so drawn up that it had the necessary flexibility to adapt and change in response to the realities of the situation obtaining in each and every scheme in operation. This step was devised to overcome the in-built delays in the tribals responses to a given situation.

This flexibility also served an equally important aim set up in the totality of planned development in respect of the *Adivasis*. This other aim transcended mere economic development of the *Adivasis* and touched the "man" for whom all these efforts were planned. In short the blueprint also covered the need to inculcate a measure of self-confidence in the *Adivasis* on which the phenomenon of self reliance rests.

Experience gained from the developmental process over the last four Plans had revealed that implementing disjointed sectoral schemes drawn up for the State as a whole does not produce any visible and/or permanent desired effect on a given local situation. It logically follows, therefore, that one of the methods to gain the desired results is to plan for a unit of an area as a whole in an integrated manner. Actually the scheme of *Ashram Shala Complex* operated in the *Adivasi* areas of the State for the last couple of years was based on this concept and its potentialities had led the Government to choose and expand the "area approach" concept for application in respect of *Adivasi* development. Thus an Ashram Shala Complex was to be the basic spatial unit of planning which was to be geographically connected with a Growth Centre to facilitate provision of low order infrastructural facilities to about six units of such complexes. Besides providing basic economic facilities, these Growth Centres were also to expose the *Adivasis* to more sophisticated metheods of production processes.

A new melded instrument for credit and marketing in the cooperative fold was being forged to tackle the problem of exploitation of the *Adivasis* at the hands of money-lenders and traders. This instrument was to cover all the facets of economic life of the Adivasis and as a supplemental measure an enactment banning money-lending as also purchase and sale of specified items by any agency other than the specified one was introduced in the tribal areas.

Machinery for implementing Plan schemes is as important as the approach and contents of the planned schemes. To obviate the necessity of approaching many agencies on the part of an Adivasi on the one hand and to facilitate smoothness in functioning of the whole planning apparatus on the other obviously means the formation of a single-line authority in the sub-Plan areas. With this aim in view provision of separate and independent tribal authorities was contemplated.

Thus the sub-Plan hinged upon a separate Tribal authority for plan implementation, on the melded credit and marketing instruments for the removal of exploitation and catering to the basic economic needs, upon the Growth Centres and Ashram Shala

Complexes for the provision of infrastructural and extension facilities and upon other well-tried schemes providing wells, pumps, electricity, vocational training and so on.

The details of the sub-Plan were worked out area by area with the advice and consent of the local *Adivasi* leadership. Obviously this process took some more time and when it was completed the final sub-Plan document with data and details emerged.

Thinking on the subjects listed below which crystallized in due course covered the following basic principles

(i) Principle of non-divertibility;
(ii) Principle of non-lapsability; and
(iii) Excise Policy
(iv) Strategy for the development of primitive tribes and extremely backward tribal groups.

Principle of Non-divertibility

The disparity between the vocality and effectiveness of tribal leadership, especially at the district level, vis-a-vis non-tribal leadership as well as comparatively poorer ability of tribal beneficiaries to absorb Plan benefit, has led to a very valid fear that even if certain schemes are specifically framed and ostensibly operated for the benfit of the tribal, in actual practice, there is always a serious danger of at least a portion of end-benefits getting diverted to non-tribals. This fear had been voiced before the Steering Committee by tribal beneficiaries on various occasions. In fact, one of the principle *raison dêtre* for framing the Tribal sub-Plan is ensuring of reservation of benefits exclusively for the tribals.

After a careful analysis of the situation, it was realized that if there is a dilution in the top authority on the deployment of Plan funds, principally by placement of block funds at the disposal of various development dapartments or field agencies for a detailed implementation of the Plan schemes, the possibility of a conscious or otherwise, leakage of benefits to non-tribals increases. Even if this is somehow prevented and a unified top-level authority takes charge of the detained development of funds, the need for a constant close watch and a continuous monitoring cannot be over-emhasized.

One of the practical measures for ensuring reservation of benefits exclusively for the tribals is the mechanics of setting up a separate "major head" in the Budget document for this purpose. Thus, once a Plan frame and resource mobilization and allocation therefor is approved by the Cabinet and when for translation of this decision annual sectoral provisions are made in the Budget, irrespective of the sector under which funds have been provided for in the budget for the specific purpose of the Tribal sub-Plan, all such funds should be pooled under the special major head. The control over the special major head will rest with the high power authority incharge of the deployment of the Tribal Sub-Plan funds and consequently no diversion of these funds without active concurrence of the high-power body would be feasible.

Under the existing practice, if funds were sanctioned for, say, irrigation, or for that matter, say, roads, under the sub-Plan, these funds would be shown under the particular major head of the respective Development Department and if any conscious or otherwise diversion of part of these funds occurs, the sub-Plan implementation authority would come to know of it only too late. Whereas, if a separate major head for this sub-Plan is set up in the Budget document, then, if the Development Department, or, for that matter, any field agency, desires to divert these funds for any other sectoral activity not covered in the sub-Plan then it will not be able to do so without the conscious and prior approval of the sub-Plan authority.

This methodology was discussed at New Delhi on April 4 and 5, 1975, and recommended by the Government of India to all State Governments. Maharashtra was the first State which took steps in this direction. We were told that certain other States, especially Bihar, Madhya Pradesh, Orissa and Uttar Pradesh had proposed to take immediate steps in the direction. The Planning and Finance Departments in Maharashtra approved of setting up of such a major head and the Accountant General had been formally moved to allot a suitable major head. Whereupon the Rs. 15 crore fund reserved for the 1975-76 sub-Plan was replaced under that major head and a drawal of these funds then was to be operated under the sanction of the controlling department, viz. the Social Welfare Department.

Principle of Non-lapsability

It has been the general experience over the last four plan periods that despite best efforts, the actual implementation of schemes, as may be estimated for a given financial year, falls short of the target and consequently a portion of the allocated funds remains unspent and at the close of a financial year such funds lapse to the detriment of successful completion of such schemes. A method for partial correction of such a situation has been developed by means, of a concept of continuing a scheme under which in the following year's budget out of the total provision available in the required sector, certain amounts, depending upon need and resource availability, are reserved for completion of such works. However, this method is neither foolproof nor absolutely scientific because obviously, in the next year's reservations, a fresh consideration of inter-se priority of schemes will enter and the fate of continuance of such an incomplete scheme will hang in the balance.

The Government of India realized that to a large degree so far as the sub-Plan is concerned, since we are working in an area without precedent; and since in a number of schemes the rate of implementation will be slow, situations of non-achievement of estimated rates of implementation, an envisaged in any Annual Plan, will multiply. Unless, therefore, a built-in corrective is provided, despite our earnest desires, the actual implementation of the Plan will fall far short of the desired objective. Nevertheless, this situation was corrected by introduction of the principle of non-lapsability of approved funds from year to year, subject to the end parameters of sectoral allocation for the entire sub-Plan period. The Government of India, therefore, proposed to introduce this principle so far as the Central Assistance component was concerned.

In the meeting held at New Delhi on April 4 and 5, 1975, it was urged that the State Government may adopt a similar procedure, so far as State sector allocations for the sub-Plan are concerned.

Mechanics of non-lapsability were to be as follows:

In the event of partial non-absorption of funds estimated and approved for any given Plan-year an automatic credit to that extent will be given to that sector in the succeeding financial year's Plan allocation. It hardly needs to be said that this procedure will be within the upper limit of the total sectoral allocation for the entire Plan period. This device in practice will do away with the concept and constraints of somehow managing to finish actual implementation of a given scheme and, therefore, consequential booking of expenditure (which leads to more than one case of hurry and unimaginative haste of booking expenditure around March 31 every year) by March 31 of that financial year. This will ensure that the pace of implementation of schemes can be more realistic and the actual booking of expenditure can be more purposive thus avoiding infructuous expenditure. It also ensures removal of the element of uncertainty in the matter of completion of schemes which remain incomplete at the end of a given financial year.

In pure budgetary theory, it really means a total commitment on the part of the State Government at the beginning of the Tribal sub-Plan to an irrevocable decision (unforeseen situation, an act of God including) regarding the gross size of resource deployment from the State sector for the entire sub-Plan period. This, in other words, means that once the State Government commits itself to a decision of the total size of the State sector's deployment for the entire sub-Plan period, then the temporary ways and means constraints will not adversely affect the year to year allocation of funds for the sub-Plan sector-wise and also shall not affect the gross deployment for the whole sub-Plan over the entire sub-Plan period.

It is realized that this concept places an added constraint on the annual flexibility of the total State resources in a given year for deployment of Plan effort as a whole in favour of the Tribal Sub-Plan. It also means that if in a particular year there is a marginal shortfall in the State's total resources against an estimate which may have been cast for that year when the State's total Fifth Five Year Plan frame was approved, such a constraint would not affect the availability of funds, so far as the approved sub-Plan is concerned; and in turn it would amount to a temporary sacrifice during that year on the part of the general sector in favour of the Tribal sector. It is felt that such a temporary sacrifice in a given year is more than due to the tribals in view of the enormous gap in development. The Steering Committee, therefore, strongly recommended adoption of this principle of non-lapsability in the matter of sub-Plan.

Excise Policy

The question as to what should be the Excise Policy during the Tribal Sub-Plan period in relation to the sub-Plan areas had been gone into in great detail by a high power body at the Government of India level and the Central Cabinet had approved of a broad strategy.

Broadly, it means:

(a) So far as vend shops for manufactured liquor are concerned, all such vend shops in the tribal areas will be closed down;
(b) The restrictions on production of home-brewed forms of liquor traditional to the tribal communities shall be totally removed, so far as tribals are concerned, and they may be allowed to freely produce such liquor and consume it which includes local village distribution, but precludes inter-village sale; and
(c) So far as tapping of toddy trees is concerned, the licences to tap toddy shall be issued only to the tribals in the sub-Plan areas.

The basic idea underlying this proposition was that vendors of hard liquor unconscionably improve their sales and thereby exploit the ignorant and weak tribal communities and, therefore, by legal closure of such vend shops the tribal can be saved from exposure to such forms of exploitation. However, the fact that tribal communities universally have a custom of imbibing softer forms of alcoholic beverages, and howsoever we may so desire, their present levels of development will cause more problems by introducing a total blanket prohibition amongst them. Therefore, constraint of production and consumption of home-brewed liquor should be removed. The exploitation of toddy trees if left to non-tribal contractors is capable of becoming another source of explotation and, therefore, tapping of toddy trees is desired to be restricted only to the tribals.

The Government of Gujarat which is weeded to a strong prohibition policy had, it is understood, not accepted the Government of India's recommendation and they proposed to pursue a policy of total prohibition. In Maharashtra they revised the approach on this subject in 1963. They have accepted total prohibition as a final ideal, but simultaneously have accepted a hard practical reality, especially in relation to the unconscionable growth of illicit liquor trade, consequent to the sudden introduction of prohibition. There is no doubt that the present policy of the State Government in relation to weaker alcoholic beverages like beer and todday as well as in relation to cheapening of certain hard liquors had resulted in a salutary reduction in the illicit liquor trade. It is equally true that the tribal leadership, at least in some places, have expressed a desire that so far as their particular villages are concerned, they would like introduction of total prohibition. The approach in Maharashtra was therefore that of broadly accepting the recommendations made by the Central Government. Wherever in a given particular village, a local elected representative by a formal resolution so requests, to the extent of that tribal village total prohibition will be introduced.

Strategy for the Development of Primitive Tribes and Extremely Backward Tribal Groups

While conceding that the tribal communites as a whole are way behind certain non-tribal communities in the pace of development, the Government of India, in their guidelines, have recognized that even amongst the tribals there are isolated small groups who are extremely backward and even occasionally at primitive levels of either hunting and food-gathering or in a very few cases at the level of the Stone Age.

In the guidelines for the Tribal Sub-Plan, a recommendation has been made for devising of special programmes for such particularly primmtive groups, if any,. in a given State. The Government of India, in the Ministry of Home Affairs, had appointed a special technical group of anthropological experts to identify such groups of primitive tribals. The Government of India recognises such groups as primitive tribal groups. Fortunately, a preponderant majority of the tribals in Maharashtra are at a stage of development far above the primitive level. The only groups of tribals which had been so identified for this purpose, in Maharashtra, are those of Madia-Gonds, mainly in Chandrapur (presently in Gadchiroli district) and due to certain economic reasons, perhaps, we may include another small groups of Katkaris in Thana and Kolaba districts. The *Koalms* from Yeotmal district and Kinwat were added later. The total number of Madia Gonds is extremely small, less than 5,000, against the total population of tribals (3 million).* The number of the Katkaris is equally small, though larger than the Madia Gonds. It will be difficult to think of and provide for special programmes in the general frame of the sub-Plan for these people.

Expert teams for making a special on-the-spot study to identify

*In fact the population of Madia Gonds is more than these Government figures. It should be around 50,000.

the immediate problems of these groups, therefore, were to be constituted and on the basis of their reports special programmes for these groups of people were to be devised. It had been indicated by the Government of India that additive support from the Government of India component for these programmes can be expected from the Central Government. Tentatively a gross ad hoc reservation of, say, Rs. 50 lakhs for such special programmes, as may be devised for these groups was initially made. This was State sector additive for these people in the sense that benefits flowing from the general Tribal Sub-Plan frame would be available to these special primitive groups of people also.

Sub-Plan and Development of the Tribal as a Man

Preparation of a sub-Plan to improve the levels of living of *Adivasi* communities though important will fail if it confines itself merely to this limited aspect of economic well-being. The sub-Plan must aim and transcend the mere physical well-being of an *Adivasi* and touch the more important aspect of the all-round development of a tribal as a man. After all the final target in any development process in any system is creating conditions in which a man lives richer, varied and happy life. Thus the very word development gets the connotation of a different hue and any sub-Plan must take this aspect into account. He must wish to live a fuller and better life.

Many and varied historical and social factors have acted and reacted to keep the tribals away from the mainstream of the Indian community and these very reasons have helped in strengthening the walls of isolation and keeping the tribals cut off from the general populace. This isolation has no doubt created a tremendous sense of diffidence and an extraordinary sense of fear amongst these tribals. Naturally, any system which aims at special efforts to develop a tribal must release forces which would create a high degree of self-confidence and inculcate an equally large measure of fearlessness amongst the *Adivasis*.

Release of such forces is bound to lead to environmental changes which will initiate the process of building up an effective leadership of sustained vigour, strong will and inherent strength amongst the *Adivasis*.

The sub-Plan could itself be a first step on the road to development of the tribal as a man if the tribals and their present leaders are associated in the totality of the Plan process. Action in this direction has already been taken by associating the tribals at the preparation stage of the sub-Plan. Moreover, at the implementation stage they are to be associated through the Advisory Committees proposed at the different levels of Plan implementation.

A reading of the administrative set-up for the Plan implementation will reveal that with the induction of a proper monitoring system in the set-up itself the responses of tribal leaders and beneficiaries about each and every scheme will be immediately picked up and relayed upwards right up to the Steering Committee with a view to reshaping or totally discarding schemes which are not proving beneficial. This flexibility factor will itself help the training of tribal leaders and beneficiaries by associating them with the schemes under operation. Besides, specific training courses for tribal beneficiaries and their leaders were also proposed in the sub-Plan.

Recommendation of the Working Group

The Working Group on Tribal Development During Medium Term Plan (1978-83) appointed by the Ministry of Home Affairs, in its report (July 1978), had categorically pointed out that, "with the level of financial investments moving up, administrative unpreparedness has appeared as an important constraint in purposive utilization of resources. . . . The establishment of a single line of command, organic integration of programmes in the field, and effective delegation of powers to the project authorities have been agreed to in principle but remain to be fully implemented. In some States even the first steps have not been taken".[1] The Group has gone further and made a very pertinent recommendation for a number of schemes for different target groups like SFDA, MFAL, DPAP, which under the new concept of Integrated Rural Development have been put on a common base. Wherever such programmes are taken up in the Tribal Sub-Plan areas, the Group has recommended that "all such special progammes should be inter-woven within the ITDP frame".[2] Uptil now (1992) this has not been done.

Among other recommendations of the working Group the following sound more urgent and interesting to those concerned with Development Administration.[3]

(i) The personnel system here should be simple with a clear

chain of command and de-overspecialized. The personal involvement of "sensitive individuals" is stressed. Orientation of personnel and adequate compensation and physical facilities, says the Group, should now be "urgently provided";

(ii) Adaptive research, large-scale field trials of proven techniques and identification of thrust programmes for each area based on the agro-climatic peculiarities of the particular tribal areas, have been advocated;

(iii) Setting up of autonomous colleges in the tribal areas with special help from the University Grants Commission is also welcome suggestion. (In Madhya Pradesh under the able guidance of Dr. B.D. Sharma, the then Tribal Commissioner and Secretary, Tribal and Harijan Welfare Department of the Government of M.P., the first autonomous college in M.P. was started at Jagdalpur.);

(iv) Infrastructural development like all-weather links to market centres, rural electrification with a view to lift irrigation, and provision of telecommunication facilities had been recommended;

(v) A "quick" survey to assess the nutrition status in the area and an even geographical spread of health services with the help of the All-India Institute of Medical Sciences, New Delhi, was suggested; and

(vi) The Group felt that the programmes for primitive groups, who are unable to adjust to the new situation, had been "slow to pick". They required the services of sensitive individuals which can be better provided by voluntary organizations. This programme will need special attention and a flexible approach.

So far as the process of change is concerned, what is good in their society and culture needs to be strengthened. Encouragement to the tribal dialects, promotion of their arts and crafts, creation of a zest for living through their dance, music and other recreational activities, augmentation of their spirit of cooperation and self-reliance and love for nature are some steps in this direction.[4]

If this approach is accepted, it becomes the responsibility of the administrator to "realize the forces working in a tribal group and adapt them to meet the new challenges. Such an adaptation would mean that there are no lost generations and that whatever is of permanent value in the older way of life is poured into the total stream of human culture. With the process of acculturation, conflict is bound to arise-between the tribal culture and the new dominant force working on it and between the old and the young. Imitation and assimilation of the dominant culture is but natural".[5]

In areas where the tribals are as yet more sensitive to change, the administrators must be cautious and avoid imposing schemes which would not be acceptable or are likely to replace what they (the tribals) consider right. They should not interfere with the process of growth but should guide and lessen the conflict so that the inevitable dialectics is paced off to help people to grow into maturity. It is for imaginative administrators to overcome the intensity of the conflict by isolating individual factors and preventing generalization and a consequent emotional upsurge.[6]

The functional virtues of sensitive and pragmatic administrators can be the most helpful factors in solving various tribal problems which form the chief message of this endeavour.

REFERENCES

1. G.O.I. Ministry of Home Affairs, *Report of the Working Group on Tribal Development during Medium-Term Plan*, 1978-83, New Delhi, July, 1978, p.ii.
2. *Ibid.*, pp. 67-68
3. *Ibid.*, pp. i-vi.
4. R.N. Haldipur, "Problems of Administration of Tribals of North-East India," *Vanyajati*, April, 1979, Vol. XXVII, No.2;
5. *Ibid.*, p.19.
6. *Ibid.*, pp. 19-20.

5

TRIBAL SUB-PLAN IN MAHARASHTRA STATE : A Model

THE 1971 Census had returned about 31 lakh *Adivasis* (tribals) in Maharashtra. Due to some constitutional difficulties this number excludes quite a few *Adivasis* staying mainly in some districts of Vidarbha.

In the last two decades of Planned development many schemes for Adivasi development were implemented. Nevertheless, these schemes had no appreciable effect due to peculiar geographical, economic and social conditions pertaining to *Adivasis*.

In the background of the above situation it was decided to chalk out a sub-Plan for Adivasi development so that this developmental effort could be put through with sufficient vigour and speed to ensure reasonable success in the development of *Adivasis*.

The task of framing the problems facing the *Adivasis* and devising of schematic solutions for the same to form part of the sub-Plan were entrusted to a Steering Committee under the Chairmanship of Shri M.D. Choudhari, Minister of Finance, Maharashtra State, vide Government Resolution No. DPB-1474-P, dated June 13, 1974. The other members of the Committee were:

(1) Minister for Finance	Chairman
(2) Minister for Social Welfare	Member
(3) Minister of State for Planning	Member
(4) Minister of State for Rural Development	Member
(5) Dy. Minister for Social Welfare	Member
(6) Member, State Planning Board (Shri L.N Bongirwar)	Member
(7) Secretary to Government, Planning Department	Member

(8) Secretary to Government, Rural Development Department — Member

(9) Secretary to Government Social Welfare, Cultural Affairs, Sports and Tourism Department — Member-Secretary

The Steering Committee initially contacted Adivasi leaders and social workers engaged in Adivasi field, management of financial and other institutions so also government departmental heads engaged in the planning processes through a questionnaire based on the Adivasi problems and their probable solutions with a view to eliciting thier opinion. A tour of the Adivasi areas was the next step taken by the Committee which was followed by a series of discussions with the Adivasis and their leaders and also concerned departmental heads. At this stage a broad outline of the sub-Plan emerged which was discussed with the Planning Commission, major financial institutions and also the Government of India. On the basis of their reactions a draft sub-Plan was prepared. This draft was finally discussed in a seminar of the Adivasis and their leadership and the same was approved by almost all the participants. Thus by involving the Adivasis themselves in the process of preparation of the sub-Plan and tempering the demands and felt needs of the Adivasis by consulting various agencies and departments to find out the feasibility of the offered solutions, a large degree of success and feasibility is tried to be built in the sub-Plan.

Sub -Plan Area and Resource Mobilization in Maharashtra

(A) Tribal Sub-Plan Area

The State's tribal population in 1981 was 57.72 lakhs which constituted about 9.19 per cent of the population. The State ranks fifth in the country according to the size of the tribal population and shares about 8 per cent of the tribal population of the country.

The tribal area in the State is mostly concentrated in two distinct belts, viz, (1) Sahyadri belt, and (2) Gondvana belt with the Satpuda hills forming part of both the belts. According to the population concentration these two belts can be further categorized on the basis of:

(a) talukas where the overall population of the Adivasis exceeds 50 per cent (Category-I);
(b) talukas where the overall population does not exceed 50 per cent but the total number of villages in such an administrative unit having population of Adivasis in excess of 50 per cent is predominant (Category-II);
(c) tribal areas not covered under categories I and II above but where tribal development blocks have been started (Category III); and
(d) tribal areas not covered under categories I, II and III but where it has been proposed to start Tribal Development Blocks (Category IV).

The tribal areas falling under these four categories were selected as sub-Plan areas of the State.

Categorywise location of the tribal areas falling in the two distinct belts as also the tribes located therein is as under:

(a) *Sahyadri Belt*: The tribal areas in Thana, Nasik, Dhulia, Poona, Ahmednagar and Kolaba districts are covered under this belt (See Table 5.1)

The tribals found in this belt are Koli-Mahadev, Varli, Kokna, Thakur, Kathodi, Koli Malhar, Koli Dhor, Dubla, Bhils, Gamit, Pardhi, Dhodia and Naikda. Eighty-two per cent of the tribal population from the selected tribal sub-Plan area is in this belt.

(b) *Gondwana Belt*: The tribal areas in the districts of Amravati, Chandrapur*, Nagpur, Bhandara, Yeotmal and Nanded fall in this belt (see Table 5.1).

The Gond, Andh, Kolam, Pardhan, Halba, Korku, Dhanka, Randhawa and Kavar tribes reside in this belt and they constitute 18 per cent of the tribal population of the selected tribal area.

The sub-plan area covers all the scheduled area in the State excepting 31 villages in Jalgaon district.

The number of villages falling under the selected sub-Plan area adds up to 6816 as shown in Table 5.1.

(B) Resource Mobilization

The districtwise sub-plan outlays are as under: The Government

* Now distributed in Chandrapur and Gadchiroli districts.

TABLE 5.1 : Villages falling under the selected sub-plan area

Sr. No.	Name of the District	Number of Villages in category I	II	III	IV	Total
1.	Thana	336	335	–	294	985
2.	Kolaba	–	–	–	98	98
3.	Nasik	299	398	116	–	813
4.	Dhulia	504	419	118	–	1041
5.	Ahmednagar	–	153	–	–	153
6.	Poona	–	–	119	21	140
7.	Nanded	–	–	–	59	59
8.	Amravati	335	–	–	–	335
9.	Yeotmal	–	–	129	377	506
10.	Nagpur	–	–	–	97	97
11.	Bhandara	–	–	–	282	282
12.	Chandrapur	650	949	153	555	2307
	Total	2124	2274	635	1783	6816

vide Annexure II of Planning Department Circular No. FFP (v) 1073/P-3 dated 18-7-1973, has laid down the method by which it has allocated financial resources to each district for the Fifth Five Year Plan. After suitable modifications in respect of all the concerned districts excepting Dhulia the same is used to arrive at the financial quantum that is proposed to be kept aside for the sub-plan. The modifications are as under:

(a) Allocation on Population Basis: 60 per cent

The percentage of population covered by the selected tribal areas in a district is used for arriving at the share of the tribal areas under this head. As, for example, under this head Thana district is allotted Rs. 32.61 crores while the population covered in the selected tribal areas in this district is 38 per cent of the district's total population. Thus the share of the tribal area under this head is calculated at 38 per cent of the total allocation for the district under this head. This works out to Rs. 12.39 crores.

(b) SC, ST, Budhist Population: 5 per cent

The percentage share of the Scheduled Tribe population of the selected tribal areas in the total Scheduled Castes, Scheduled Tribes and Budhist population in a district is used to arrive at the tribal area's share under this head. In Dhulia district, for example, the Scheduled Tribe population of the selected tribal area is 4.29 lakhs, i.e. 63 per cent of the district's Scheduled Caste, Scheduled Tribe and Budhist population. Thus out of Rs. 4.59 crores under this head, the allocation for the selected tribal areas will be Rs. 2.89 crores.

(c) Urban Population: 5 per cent

The share of the selected tribal area under this head is arrived at by finding out the proportion of urban population in the selected tribal area in the district's total urban population and then apportioning this proportion from the said head. As for example, the urban population in the selected tribal areas of Nasik district constitutes 3.5 per cent of the district's total urban population and therefore, its share out of Rs. 2.59 crores under this head amounts to Rs. 0.09 crores.

(d) Geometric Mean of Agricultural Backwardness Per Hectare and Per Worker : 5 per cent

Though the difference in the level as well as standard of living between the tribal and non-tribal population cannot be easily quantified it is assumed to be one-half for the purpose of this exercise. On the basis of this assumption the per capita allocation under this head in a district is doubled for a tribal. As for example, the over-all per capita outlay under this head for Ahmednagar district amounts to Rs. 14 and thus the same for a tribal is taken to be Rs 28. After this doubling, the outlay for the total population in the selected tribal area is calculated on the basis of this doubled per capita outlay. Thus the per capita outlay on this score for the selected area's population in Ahmednagar district amount to Rs. 0.44 lakhs.

(e) Road and Railway Length per sq. km. and Per Lakh Population : 5 per cent

As per (d) above

(f) Irrigation Backwardness : 5 per cent

As per (d) above.

(g) Industrial Backwardness

As per (d) above.

(h) Rural Population of Coastal District

The proportion of rural population of coastal district falling in the selected tribal area out of the total such rural population in the district is used in allocationg finances under this head. As for example, this proportion in Thana district is 60 per cent and thus the allocation under this head for the selected tribal areas is Rs. 3.58 crores.

(i) Drought-prone Rural Population : 2 per cent

Same as (h) above.

(j) Forest Areas : 1.5 per cent

The proportion of forest area located in the selected tribal area of a district is used for apportioning the allocation for the tribal area in a district. As for example, in Chandrapur district cent per cent of the forest area falls in the selected tribal area. Thus the whole allocation, i.e. Rs. 5.74 crores, of this district will be allocated for the Tribal sub-Plan.

In respect of Dhulia district the weightage of tribal population therein has been used as the base for allocation in all the 10 criteria because if the same basis as is adopted for the remaining concerned districts is also applied for this district, the Tribal sub-plan allocation will overshoot the district's total fifth plan allocation.

The allocations for the Fifth Five Year Plan period and for the Annual Plan 1975-76 in the Tribal Sub-plan area are given in Table 5.2.

Quite a few Adivasis still in Primitive Stage

Most of the Adivasis in the State live in mountain ranges.

Table 5.2: The Annual Plan 1975-76 in the tribal sub-plan area

(*Rs. in crores*)

Sr. No.	Name of the District	Sub Plan		District Plan (Fifth Plan)
		Fifth Plan*	Annual Plan 1975-76	
1.	Thana	28.76	3.31	54.74
2.	Kolaba	1.52	0.17	28.94
3.	Nasik	19.85	2.29	55.17
4.	Dhulia	20.63	2.38	42.45
5.	Ahmednagar	4.06	0.47	45.81
6.	Poona	2.37	0.27	62.56
7.	Nanded	1.24	0.15	31.63
8.	Amravati	6.18	0.71	37.42
9.	Yeotmal	8.41	0.97	37.03
10.	Nagpur	2.01	0.24	42.68
11.	Bhandara	29.64	3.42	42.83
12.	Chandrapur	29.64	3.42	42.83
	Total	130.00	15.00	519.53

* includes expected Government of India allocations.

Geographically speaking they are located in the Sahyadri ranges in the west, Satpuda ranges in the north and north-east and in the Gondwana areas in the east. As mentioned earlier the Adivasis form 9.19 per cent of the State's population. This number excludes about five lakh unenumerated Adivasis located mostly in some districts of Vidarbha division. Due to the non-inclusion of certain Adivasis in the requisite constitutional provisions they have remained unenumerated.

Most of the Adivasis in the State are concentrated in pockets in the 12 districts of the State. These districts are Thana, Nasik, Dhulia, Poona, Ahmednagar and Kolaba in western Maharashtra; parts of Kinwat taluka in Nanded; and Amravati, Nagpur, Bhandara, Yeotmal and Chandrapur in the Vidarbha region.

Nearly 65 per cent of the Adivasis are agriculturists, while the majority of the remaining persons in the workforce are engaged as agricultural labour and in cottage industries. Nearly a lakh of adivasis are found in urban centres like Bombay and Poona.

The generality of the population are now conversant with the process of planning as practised for the last 20 years in India. In this period the basic infrastructure has also been laid down in the rural areas. Nevertheless on both these counts, the progress in respect of the Adivasis leaves much room for improvement. The schemes operated in this period being oriented mostly towards the generality of the population have benefited this segment of the population and has also helped them in absorbing new techniques as well the benefits flowing from the same. But unfortunately this absorption is absent in the case of the Adivasis. In the view of some experts the Adivasis are yet to cover a 50-year period to reach the existing levels of their counterparts in other areas. Some experts also hold the view that quite a few Adivasis are still in the Stone Age! It is a matter of pride that the Adivasis in Maharashtra are much advanced being agriculturists in the full sense of the word exception a handful like the Madia Gonds in Chandrapur (now in Gadchiroli) and Katkaris in western Maharashtra who were till recently at a primitive stage. Of late the Kolam have also been classified as a primitive tribe. Of course this does not mean that the Advasis are not undeveloped and all the planning effort undertaken for them must start with this premise only. Thus any plan edifice built on this premise will mean that one has to telescope the Plan process spread over a 75-year period in a much shorter time span and the national aim being 15 years, all the orientation and all the schemes of the sub-plan must achieve the goals in this given time compass.

Once the time factor and the goals are fixed it becomes useful to list out the major impediments that may hinder progress along the laid-down course, and after having isolated hindrance factors the probable solutions also could be thought of. The major impediments and the solutions therefore are as under:

(a) exploitation in all forms and the schemes to stop the same;
(b) isolation from the mainstream of community life due to communication barriers and the schemes to break the same and reorientation of the Adivasis towards assimilating modern methods of productive processes;
(c) unstable and uneconomic agriculture and the schemes to stabilze the same thus improving the levels of living of the Adivasis who mainly depend upon agriculture;
(d) lack of self-confidence and lack of vocality amongst the

Adivasis and the schemes to train them and their leadership in the process of planning; and

(e) lack of supporting economic means of livelihood and the schemes to train the Adivasis in starting the same.

Obviously the above list is not exhaustive but one will have to note that in an undeveloped economy all the schemes for total development cannot be taken up at once due to various constraints and as such priorities have to be fixed. While doing so, however, schemes which are basic and act as catalytic agents for further development within a short time span only need be selected on a priority basis.

In the background of the above aims and constraints, some basic tenets have been formulated by the Government for the sub-Plan frame. The first tenet is that instead of operating only individual-oriented schemes all the schemes will be integrated with a view to developing an area, i.e. an integrated area development approach will be followed. Secondly, while doing so the State Government's on-going area development complex (Ashram Shala) schemes will be used as a focal point in and around which an extended network culminating in a Growth Centre will be operated. This centre will make available to groups of villages basic infrastructural facilities to release economic and environmental forces required for development. Thirdly, in this spatial set-up a new institutionalized credit-cum-marketing cooperative agency will be intermeshed at appropriate points so that the aim of the said agency of breaking the money-lender-cum-trader complex by touching the total economic life of an Adivasi will have a reasonable chance of success. Fourthly, operating various developmental schemes in an integrated manner over a compact area within a given time span to succeed will need an administrative structure which will devote its entire apparatus at all the levels and at all the time towards this purpose. And with this aim in view so also to minimize the need of an Adivasi to approach many agencies for his multifarious requirements the operation of the sub-Plan will be entrusted to an independent tribal authority. Lastly, the on-going schemes such as wells, provision of electricity, health facilities and so on will be restructured and reoriented to suit individuals as well as area needs.

Exploitative Practices and Corrective Measures

The exploitation of the Adivasis in Maharashtra takes various forms. Basically, however, the roots of exploitation are seen to have gone deep in the basic economic activity undertaken by the Adivasis, viz. agriculature. Rich fertile soil in combination with total ignorance on the part of the Adivasis about the mechanics of production processes and absence of any single agency to cater to the economic needs connected with agriculture has exposed the Adivasis to the machinations of a credit-marketing-trading nexus operated by unscrupulous and rapacious middlemen. This exposure had led to heavy indebtedness and transfer of the only productive asset, viz. land, to the non-Adivasis. The total effect of this operation over a number of years has brought about total stagnation in the economic activity of the Adivasis and reduced them to the level of serfs with no hope of a release from the dutches of this evil nexus.

Thus the measures to remove exploitative practices will mean measures to restore lands illegally transferred, measures to scale down past debts, measures to avoid recurrence of indeptedness, measures to ensure fair price for the produce brought for sale by the Adivasis, and measures to create an institutionalized structure which besides giving credit and marketing facilities offers extension services in the field of agriculture. All these measures will release the Adivasi from the bondage of the middlemen and help him to consolidate such release by the offer of extension services.

In the following paragraphs measures for restoration of lands, measures for scaling down of debts and stoppage of money-lending and trading by any person other than a notified one and measures for institutionalised credit-cum-marketing structure are explained.

Land Alienation

The following two measures have been taken by the Government of Maharashtra for restoration to the adivasis of their land which has gone into the hands of non-Adivasis, either as a result of valid or invalid transfers:

(1) Maharashtra Land Revenue Code and Tenancy Laws (Amendment) Act, 1974 (Mah. Act No. XXXV of 1974) which replaces Maharashtra Order No. XIII of 1974. This Act has

come into force with effect from 6-7-1974.

(2) Maharashtra Restoration of lands to Scheduled Tribes Act 1974.

The Maharashtra Land Revenue Code and Tenancy Law (Amendment) Act, 1974, provides for restoration to the tribals of all their lands which have gone into the hands of non-tribals as a result of invalid transfers, i.e. transfers effected in contravention of the law, no compensation whatsoever is to be paid to the non-tribals in respect of the land so restored to the tribals.

According to the provisions of Section 36 of the Maharashtra Land Revenue Code 1966 (as it stood before it was amended by the above amending Act) tribal areas were required to be notified in the official Gazette and occupancies of tribals in such notified areas were not to be transferred without the previous sanction of the Collector. Where a transfer is effected in contravention of the aforesaid provisions the tribal transferor could apply to the Collector for restoration of the land within two years from the date of transfer. No advantage of this provision, however, appears to have been taken by the large number of the tribal transferors and the transfers which were not made with the previous sanction of the Collector have continued to remain as invalid transfers. In the non-notified areas, however, no such sanction was necessary, and the transfer of occupancies by tribals without the sanction of the Collector were valid, unless they contravened the provisions of any other law in force.

By the amendments made to the aforesaid Section 36 by the above-mentioned amending Act, the provision for notifying tribal areas has been deleted and the scope of the aforesaid section has been extended to the entire State. The result is that any tribal will come within the purview of the amending Act, irrespective of whether he is a resident of the motified area or not. Even so, as the incidence of invalid transfers is more in the notified areas only, for the reasons stated above, the effect of the amending act will be felt mostly in those areas.

The Maharashtra Restoration of Lands to Scheduled Tribes Act, 1974, which came into force in May, 1975 provides for the restoration to the tribals of their lands validly transferred (including the purchases made under the Tenancy Law) to non-tribals between the period from April 1, 1957 to July 6, 1974. The scope of this Act also extends to the entire State and any valid transfer effected by a tribal in favour of a non-tribal within the aforesaid period comes within its ambit irrespective of whether the transferor Adivasis is a resident of the notified area or not.

The compensation to be paid by the tribal to the non-tribal in respect of the land restored to him under the provisions of this Act is as under:

(a) In respect of land, other than the land purchased by the non-tribal under the Tenancy Law–
   (i) 48 times the assessment of the land or the amount of consideration paid by the non-tribal transferee for acquisition of the land, whichever is less, plus; and
   (ii) the value of improvements made by the non-tribal on the land, as may be determined by the Collector. The expression "improvements" includes drainage works, Bandharas, wells, etc., and also trees planted on the land.
(b) In respect of lands purchased under the Tenancy Law, the amount of purchase price or a proportionate part thereof paid by the non-tribal transferee.

The amount of compensation in both these categories is to be paid in 12 annual instalments with simple interest at four-and-half per cent per annum. The problem regarding transfer of land from Adivasis to non-Adivasis is predominant in the district of Dhulia. According to the reports earlier received in this district there are 1,198 valid transactions in which 7,080 acres of land has been transferred to non-Adivasis (apparently this does not include sales under the Tenancy Act). Besides there are 2,693 invalid transactions. If the area involved in valid sales is any indication about 18,000 acres of land would be involved in such transactions. The other districts in which transfers of land from Adivasis to non-Adivasis have been reported are Thane (valid 46, invalid 50), and Chandrapur (valid 25, invalid 16). Invalid transfers might have also occurred in other districts such as Nasik, Yoetmal, Amravati, etc., where there is a mixed population of Adivasis and non-Adivasis and these will have also to be dealt with under the provision of the Maharashtra Act No. XXXV of 1974.

As already pointed out above, no compensation is to be paid in respect of the land involved in invalid transfers.

Scaling Down of Debts, Stoppage of Money-Lending and Trading by Non-notified Persons

To achieve the purpose mentioned in the title given above, "The Maharashtra Prevention of Exploitation of Tribal Act 1975" was enacted for the sub-Plan areas which was given effect in 1976. The salient features of the above named Act are as under:

As from the appointed day all standing contracts, wherever in writing or otherwise, which are essentially of the nature of money-lending (including bonded labour) where the borrower is an Adivasi shall stand abrogated and all charges, easements and right to immoveable and moveable property of a borrower tribal which may have been created or which may exist consequent to the contracts mentioned above shall automatically stand vacated as from the appointed day and from that day all charges, easements and rights existing in favour of the lender on the immoveable and moveable property of the borrower shall so far as the lender is concerned stand vacated and the said charges, easements and rights shall stand transferred in favour of a notified agency.

As from the appointed day, it shall be unlawful to enter into any transaction with a tribal, where the transaction is essentially of the nature of money-lending, irrespective of the fact whether as a consequence to the said contract any charge, easement or right is created on the immoveable or moveable property of a borrower tribal in favour of the lender, by any person other than an agency or a person who may be so notified under this Act.

As from the appointed day, it shall be unlawful for any person to enter into any contract, whether in writing or otherwise, or sale, barter or transfer in any other manner of any commodity which was mentioned in a schedule produced or foregathered by a "tribal"; save by such agencies or institutions as may be notified in this behalf. The State Government may from time to time by a notification published in the official Gazette notify such produce, commodities or foregathering which may attract the provisions explained in this paragraph.

After taking the above steps the vacuum created by the same is prosposed to be filled by instituting a melded credit-cum marketing instrument the salient features of which are given below.

It does not require to be argued any longer that the release of tribals from economic and commercial exploitation and their subsequent rapid economic development require designing of a new arrangement to cater for all the economic needs of tribals.

At the outset it would be useful to enumerate broadly the principal areas of economic activities in tribal community life which, as a minima, the new arrangement must touch. They could be:

(a) Quantification and servicing of previous debts contracted from registered and unregistered lending sources;
(b) Organization and deployment of short, medium, and long-term production credit;
(c) Setting up of a sales-purchase organization to buy off all the produce or foregathering by a tribal at a fair price and, in turn, sell to him majority of his and his family's daily consumption needs including those pertaining to the lean months and provide for the annual periodic community overheads at a reasonable cost;
(d) Dissemination of technical advice for improved agronomical and other practices and the sale of supporting inputs; and
(e) Slowly inculcate banking habits, thrift and financial discipline in the tribals.

It is obvious that to service vigorously the aforesaid five major areas, an effective and flexible new instrument has to be forged to ensure a reasonable chance of achieving a break through in the tribal economy.

There are two major aspects of the proper designing of the required new instrument, viz. structural and financial.

Structural Arrangement

Against the back drop of the areas of activities that the new instrument will have to tackle, it need not be unnecessarily laboured that due to extremely low level of ability of available local organizational and managerial skills, a very high degree and extent of such skills will have to be provided for, at least in the beginning, to make such an instrument achieve the desired results. This presupposes an outlay on overheads much in excess of a normal multi-purpose cooperative credit society to start with. Here one cardinal point cannot be overlooked. In the last analysis, the whole endeavour is to release environmental forces which will gradually induce the desired level of self-confidence in tribals to enable them to run their own affairs, and, as such, any new instrument must provide for the participation of the tribal beneficiaries in the management ultimately leading to total takeover of the management by the tribals.

The State had already set up a Co-operative Tribal Development Corporation (TDC) at the State level primarily to implement commercial programmes for the benefit of the tribals, as well as to undertake developmental activities for them. Although the objectives of the Tribal Development Corporation in the background of its financial and other limitations were overambitious and were not fully defined, it could be usefully converted into a middle-level field agency for catering to all the commercial and economic needs of the tribals as further explained below. This meant that structurally the Tribal Development Corporation will have to be reorganized and theoretically it will have to shed totally its developmental function like organization and running of Ashram Shalas. These and other development activities could be taken over by the new sub-Plan authorities. This will help in reducing multiplicity of agencies that a tribal has to deal in sub-Plan areas.

After fitting in of the existing institution (TDC) in the proposed pattern and to enable one to dovetail the remaining pieces with the new pattern, it will be useful to know the sub-Plan's spatial organizational spread.

The most common size of a village located in the selected sub-Plan area was about 105 families with around 575 people of which, approximately, 60 families with 310 persons are tribals. The basic organization for the sub-Plan areas will be a growth centre. A growth centre will cover between 25,000 and 30,000 persons, or 5,000 to 5,300 families, out of which tribal families will be between 2,700 and 3,000 with a population of around 15,000 to 16,000. These families will be spread over four to five Ashram Shalas, each covering about 10 villages with about 1,000 families of around 6,000 souls.

The above facts in regard to tribal orgnization will suggest that the lowest tier in the proposed new arrangement will have to be a growth centre. This will help compensate the comparative lack of entrepreneurial ability and managerial skill vis-a-vis the newer challenges of organizing a flexible instrument to run disparate but very essential economic activities at the grass root level. It has now been conceded (National Agriculture Commission) that for the rapid development of weaker sections in the areas where the normal pattern of cooperative agencies at the field level is weak, a more sophisticated and comprehensive organization in the shape of Farmer's Service Societies has to be conceived. A similar thought underlies the recommendation of setting up of a Rural Bank (Sarayya Commission's Report.)

However, after further analysis it will be realized that creating the new facility at a growth centre level will lead to operational difficulties due to the peculiar nature terrain of the sub-Plan area so also the far-flung locations of tribal villages. Moreover, due to the introduction of a totally different type of activity the new facility will perform, at least in the initial years, a careful nursing of member accounts will have to be undertaken by the management. All this suggests that the new facility should be offered at a level lower than the proposed growth centre and within the financial constraints. The best geographical point at which this could be done would be an area which will serve about 12,500 people. This means that there would be two societies under a growth centre.

The above exposition will logically suggest the following arrangement which could be adopted in the sub-Plan area:

(a) the new arrangement should be three-tier cooperative cridit-cum-marketing structure;
(b) the primary field agency could be a credit-cum-marketing organization at the bottom with two such units in each of the proposed growth centres. This agency could be styled as "Adivasi Cooperative Society" (ACS) and it will operate, wherever necessary, through its branches located in the Ashram Shalas coming under a growth centre's purview, the number of branches being five at the maximum and each branch covering 3,000 to 4,000 people;
(c) the present sales/purchase centres (approx. 59) operated by the Tribal Development Corporation will have to be shut down/merged and their activities taken over by the Adivasi Cooperative Society;
(d) The ACS should normally undertake the following

functions:

(i) preparation for each member a total credit portfolio comprising:

(a) short, medium, and long-term production credit requirement;

(b) debt servicing for liquidation of past debt; and

(c) provision of credit in cash and kind for consumption purposes, especially consumption requirements arising in lean months and outlays on occasional annual community overheads.

(ii) purchase of all commodities either produced or foregathered by a member; and

(iii) sale of all the basic agricultural inputs covering supply of all agricultural capital assets.

The ACS will translate this into practice by opening a composit cash credit account for each member.

(e) all the existing primary Cooperative field agencies within the operational area of an ACS will have to be merged with the ACS;

(f) for the purposes of flow of finances and refinance facilities the ACSs will be linked with the concerned* DCC Bank in respect of ST and MT loans and consumption finance; for all marketing activities other than the marketing of Minor Forest Produce the linkage will be with the concerned Taluka Purchase and Sale Union; for marketing of Minor Forest Produce the ACSs will be linked with the Tribal Cooperative Development Corporation. These middle-tier agencies and their upper linkages will be as they are obtained today in the cooperative movement of the State. Regarding long-term loan finance it has to be noted that after accepting the principle of providing all the economic needs of a tribal beneficiary at one placc it is obvious that the long-term loans should also be routed through the ACS. This will mean that the district branches of the Maharashtra State Land Development Bank will have to

* District Central Cooperative Bank.

> do their business through the ACSs by appointing the latter as their agents. Alternatively it could be visualized that even the long-term loans could be dispensed by the District Central Cooperative Banks in the sub-Plan areas.

In effect the ACSs will embrace all aspects of the sub-Plan area tribal's economic activity which will also mean cross-accounting of all their transactions through a member passbook. Through this passbook system the tribal beneficiaries will be slowly introduced to banking habits and through retention of small portions of sale moneys in favour of beneficiaries via the passbook, habit of thrift, capital formation, and self-reliance will be inculcated.

To ensure a full and complete marriage of all aspects of economic life of a tribal with this ACS, and consequently ensure the tribal's permanent freedom from usury and exploitation at the hands of rapacious private traders, some form of legal sanction will have to be secured to prevent sale in any form in favour of private or other parties (except ACS) of anything produced or foregathered by a tribal within the area of operation of an ACS. Purchase of paddy, forest produce such as gum myrabalan, cast away horns and bones, *tendu* leaves etc, have all been restricted and the tribals can now sell these only to the ACS or other agencies authorised by the Government. This has put an end to the exploitation by the traders. However, of late, due to the inefficient functioning of the ACS, poor linkage with the higher authorities in the whole structure and red-tape, the tribals are left at bay and are compelled to sell such products to traders clandestinely. This again gives rise to occasion for exploitation.

Provision of Infrastructural Facilities

It was around the year 1950-51 that the Community Development Projects were started in the country. After a lapse of some time, in tribal areas, "Tribal Development Blocks" were initiated in the Community Development Blocks. These TD Blocks were used to be financed by the Government of India. But from April 1, 1975, the Government had stopped its financial aid leaving it to the State Governments to continue with it with its own financial arrangements. While doing so the Government of India had suggested that these TD Blocks be substituted by integrated Tribal Development

Projects.

Two basic needs of the Adivasis get focussed while analysing the problems of Adivasi development. They are satisfying the immediate felt needs of the Adivasis and creating the basic infrastructural facilities as near the Adivasi as is physically possible so that the Adivasi could be exposed to the basic modern productive processes and assimilate the benefits flowing therefrom. The first need is proposed to be catered through the already existing Ashram Shala complexes. It is the satisfaction of the second need that will require a carefully thought-out solution. As already mentioned the second basic need could be satisfied by spreading the infrastructural network horizontally as well as vartically in the spatial sense so that it reaches the last link in the chain of development, viz. an Adivasi himself.

During 1954-74 a well-knit network of such facility had been created for the general population up to the taluka level and such facility was aiding the fructification of planned development at a rapid pace. At some places though this network is obtainable in the sub-Plan areas up to the taluq level, the peculiar geographical, economic, social and environmental forces operating in the Tribal Sub-Plan area makes it imperative to take it down vertically to as low a level as is financially and physically possible. Though the physical constraint can be overcome with an effective administrative set-up the financial constraint will make it well nigh impossible to take down these facilities to the desired level. It has been observed that the infrastructural facilities culminating in the taluq headquarter itself was very costly though it was realized that over a period of time this cost was well spent because it served as a catalytic agent of development the benefits of which cover the said cost with ease and help in accelerating economic growth.

Against this backdrop one will rightly opt for an Ashram Shala Complex for providing the said infrastructural facilities. However, a detailed analysis of the financial resources required to be deployed for the creation of such facility at the said point reveals that the benefit flowing from the said point could be had at a much lesser cost if this point is located in between the taluq headquarter and Ashram Shala Complex points. With this reasoning in view it has been decided that for a group of six Ashram Shala Complexes or for a population of 25,000 one Growth Centre will be created. Under one growth centre there will be two new agencies for dispensing credit and offering marketing facilities; one agency covering about 12,500 population, and below one such agency there would be three Ashram Shala Complexes each covering a population of about 3,000. This spatial set-up will at once indicate that the infrastructural facilities are vertically arranged in such a manner that the most basic primary immediate needs are arranged to be satisfied at the lowest point (Ashram Shala Complex level), a bit more complicated and yet all-embracing economic need, viz. need for credit and marketing facility will be satisfied at the next higher point, viz. at the melded instrument for credit and marketing level, and lastly the remaining infrastructural arrangements detailed below will be at the Growth Centre level.

The infrastructural facilities that will be provided at the growth centre level will consist of:

- (i) Demonstration Farms;
- (ii) Soil Testing Laboratory;
- (iii) Bazar facility;
- (iv) Forest, agro-based and other small-scale industries complex;
- (v) Multi-purpose vocational training workshop;
- (vi) Primary Health unit and rural hospital;
- (vii) ST bus stop;
- (viii) Community recreation centre;
- (ix) Godown facilities;
- (x) Inspection huts;
- (xi) Post and Telegraph Office;
- (xii) Police outpost
- (xiii) Water supply and electricity unit; and
- (xiv) Growth Centre office.

The success of the concept of the Growth Centre was obviously to depend upon the proper location of the same and it was proposed to start 15 such centres in the Annual Plan 1975-76. In due course of development the Growth Centre in its envisaged form could not be translated into reality. Though some of the facilities were provided, all of them were not brought into a compact whole. The infrastructural facilities, remained scattered in the area.

Though the Government of India had suggested adoption of Integrated Tribal Development Projects as a unit of area planning, the situation then obtaining in Maharashtra with its relatively dispersed tribal population was markedly different from that obtaining in other States with a larger degree of concentrated tribal population like Madhya Pradesh where whole districts have one-half of its population composed of tribals. It was this consideration and an additional consideration of a higher degree of expertise obtained at the district level in the matter of planning process in Maharashtra as compared to other States, that a Growth Centre was chosen as a basic unit of planning in the sub-Plan areas of Maharashtra instead of the ITDP. The other formulations around an ITDP are maintained around a Growth Centre.

Broad Outline of Other Schemes

A broad outline of other schemes is as under:

Agriculture

The following schemes will be included under this sector:

(i) training of the techniques for adoption of improved agricultural practices;
(ii) godowns for seeds and fertilizers;
(iii) crop protection;
(iv) soil conservation; and
(v) demonstration of improved farming practices.

Animal Husbandry

The stress will be on higher milk production by introducing improved breeds of cattle.

Dairy Development

Under this head schemes regarding collection of milk, breeding of better variety of milch cattle and production milk products are included.

Education

Under this head following schemes are included:

(i) supply of free books to ST pupils studying in Standards I to V;
(ii) supply of uniforms without cost to Adivasi girls studying in Standards I to V;
(iii) strengthening of inspection staff for efficient supervision of schools in the tribal sub-Plan area;
(iv) leadership training to local tribals; and
(v) preparation of textbooks in Adivasi dialects.

Technical Education

The provision for the establishment of well equipped technical and vocational institute at growth centres is proposed under this head.

Public Health

This includes establishment of Primary Health Centres and Rural Hospitals.

Communication

It is proposed to provide all-weather roads connecting Growth Centres and other points of development. In addition, bridges on rivers and culverts and small bridges on stream will be constructed.

Water Supply for Irrigation and Drinking Water

Under the irrigation schemes construction of new wells, installation of pump sets, organization of lift irrigation societies, construction of percolation and small irrigation tanks are proposed.

Drinking water facilities would be provided on a priority basis to the villages where no facility exists at the present. In addition the improvement in the existing drinking water facilities will be provided wherever necessary.

Assistance of the Ground Water Survey and Development Agency will be taken for the construction of wells.

Electrification

Electrification of Growth Centres and the surrounding villages to start with will be carried out.

Forest Development

This includes establishment of small industrial and processing units based on forest-produced raw materials. In addition the existing schemes will be continued.

Machinery for Sub-Plan Implementation

The primary objective of the planning effort for tribals as has been explained earlier is to bring them as close to the level of development of the general population as is physically feasible within a very short period of 15 years. A closer scrutiny of the existing planning machinery will reveal that the same has evolved to suit those who are geographically, economically, socially, environmentally in a different set of circumstances then the Adivasis. This is obviously so because the existing planning machinery has evolved through a process of trial-and-error spread over four Plan periods with a sharp and distinct orientation towards the level of absorption capacity and qualitative differences in the felt needs and leadership qualities obtained in the general population. Such machinery obviously will work very haltingly and at times will not be in harmony with the levels of absorption capacity, nascent leadership qualities, high levels of illiteracy and apathy observed in the Adivasis.

The above reasoning will at once indicate that in the background of area approach the Plan implementing authority in respect of sub-Plan should not be merely an agency which will put through the given schemes in a rigid manner but should be an agency which will quickly respond to the results of continuous and concurrent monitoring, which will consider the whole gamut of planning in an integrated manner, which will telescope the total Plan process right from the designing through to the implementation stage of each and every scheme in a given time span, which will avoid an Adivasi beneficiary approaching different governmental outlets to satisfy his economic and other requirements, which will be fresh in outlook and equipped with the necessary wherewithal, which will be simple to understand, which will avoid duplication and overlapping with the existing machinery, and which will possess the necessary flexibility to function both as a regulatory and developmental agency in sub-Plan areas.

The above ingredients of the sub-Plan implementing machinery will mean setting up of a powerful single-line pyramidical structure. The following structure will eminently suit the purpose.

At the top there will be a Steering Committee consisting of Government members which will be the final authority in all the matters concerning the sub-Plan and will be responsible to the Government. This step will ensure focussing of all sub-Plan activity in one authority at the government level. The actual implementation and day-to-day working of the sub-Plan will be entrusted to the Social Welfare Department assisted by the Secretary to that Department and his Secretariate staff. It will be the function of the Social Welfare Department to monitor and evaluate the sub-Plan schemes with a view to assessing its usefulness and the need to carry out changes in the same as and when required.

Below the Social Welfare Department and responsible to it will be the two tribal authorities in the field, one for Sahydri region and the other for the Gondwana region with headquarters at Nasik and Nagpur respectively. These authorities will be headed by an officer of the commissioner's rank with the necessary powers to discharge the sole responsibility in the matter of superintendence and overseeing of the sub-Plan in his jurisdiction. With a view to integrateing all the sub-Plan schemes and telescope the time span of Plan implementation all the stages in the Plan process will be focussed in this authority for which purpose high-level technical officers from concerned technical departmants will be seconded to this authority for the duration of the concerned scheme. This will obviate inter-departmental consultations and sanctions. To assist the Commissioner a small Commissionerate office will be established on a permanent basis.

Below the Commissionerates and responsible to it will be a Deputy Commissioner (Tribal) who is at present the Collector of the sub-Plan district. He will be responsible for the implementation of the sub-Plan in his district. He will continue to exercise magisterial functions also. He will be assisted by the technical staff already working under him and in case he does not have the requisite technical officer the same will be loaned from the Zilla Parishad under the relevant statutory provision.

For developmental work, the Deputy Commissioner (Tribal) will be assisted by the Adivasi Vikas Adhikari who will be incharge of a Growth Centre. Since a Growth Centre will be more on less conterminus with a TD Block the services of all the functionaries of the Panchayat Samiti right down to the village level will be requisitioned from the Zilla Parished under the relevant statutory provision of the Maharashtra Zilla Parished and Panchayat Samities Act. Since there will be two credit-cum-marketing cooperative societies in a Growth Centre area which will be offering extension services also, the superintendence of the latter function will be entrusted to the Adivasi Vikas Adhikari alongwith all the other sub-Plan schemes operated in the area of a Growth Centre. The Adivasi Vikas Adhikari will be responsible to the Deputy Commissioner (Tribal).

The regulatory functions will be carried out by the Deputy Commissioner (Tribal) with the aid of the present staff right from the village Talathi upwards, in the sub-Plan area of a district.

Below a Growth Centre level there will be two cooperative societies and further below there will be the Ashram Shala Complexes, manned by their respective staff.

The above configuration will reveal that a single line authority for sub-Plan implementation is being set up which is simple to understand, which obviates the need to approach multifarious agencies, which avoids duplication by the use of the existing machinery wherever feasible, which is armed with the necessary powers to discharge heavy responsibility, which is so staffed as to minimize delays and maximize flexibility of operation, etc. The cost of the new posts created in the Commissionerates adds up to Rs. 30 lakhs over the whole sub-Plan period which amounts to a fraction of one per cent of the total sub-Plan outlay of Rs. 130 crores.

The popular participation of tribal beneficaries and their leaders is assured in the following manner.

(i) At the State level the Tribes Advisory Council will advise the Steering Committee;

(ii) At the district level a special Executive Committee of the District Planning and Development Council with adequate tribal representation will be formed to advise the Tribal Authority in the matter of sub-plan. The Minister-in-charge of the district will be its Chairman and the Deputy Commissioner (Tribal) its Member-Secretary;

(iii) At the Panchayat Samiti level a similar body will be formed with the Sabhapati (if tribal) or tribal MLA from its area of operation as Chairman and Adivasi Vikas Adhikari as Member Secretary.

In the matter of development of the Adivasis living outside the sub-Plan areas a modified version of the existing Directorate of Tribal Welfare will be responsible for the same and this Directorate will have no functions to perform in the sub-plan areas.

There will be a definite personnel policy in regard to personnel posted in the Tribal Sub-plan areas. The main emphasis will be on the mode of selection of persons manning all the posts in the Tribal Sub-plan areas. Two selection committees were proposed for selection of all the officers of different ranks, and the job specifications etc., were worked out separately.

The State Cabinet in its meeting of May 14, 1975, approved in principle the proposed machinery for the implementation of the sub-Plan. However, the Tribal Authority was to consist of one Tribal Commissioner and the concerned Chief Executive Officer who will be designated as Deputy Commissioner (Tribal) will be responsible for the implementation of the sub-Plan in the districts instead of the District Collectors as proposed. Later, this structure was revised as shown below.

The Aftermath

The elaborate administrative machinery, right from the Special Multi-purpose Blocks and Tribal Development Blocks to the latest effort under the Tribal sub-Plan, has been based on problems identified in particular tribal areas. However, many tribal pockets are still at such a low stage of development that students of tribal development feel that the problems of development of tribal areas merit further study. Discussions in which administrators, anthropologists, subject-matter specialists and social workers come together need to be encouraged, and wherever possible, tribal leaders should also be invited to join.

Tribal development efforts acquired a new dimension at the time of formulation of the Fifth Five Year Plan when it was realized that in spite of the implementation of special tribal development programmes during the previous Plans, the progress of tribal communities was unsatisfactory, which, according to one view, was mainly due to the rigid, schematic pattern of the programmes and the inadequacy of funds. A need was, therefore, felt for a separate development approach to the problems of the tribal people in the country as a whole. The Planning Commission advocated the area development approach, and the concept of a sub-Plan for the areas with a high concentration of tribal people was adopted. The identified tribal areas in States were constituted into various Integrated Tribal Development Projects (ITDP) and detailed sectoral schemes were prepared for each project. In many States an administrative structure was evolved under a Tribal Commissioner to administer the sub-Plan projects with an Additional Commissioner (Tribal Development) at the divisional level and a Deputy Commissioner (Tribal) at the district level, who, in the Maharashtra model, is the Collector, under whom Project Officers for the various ITDPs work for their respective areas.

The whole new administration structure started functioning late, i.e. in 1976-77, and the working has not been very useful though satisfactory. The most prominent shortcoming is the lack of coordination between the functioning of these various administrative agencies which results in overlapping and duplication at the one end, and haphazard and incomplete endeavours at the other. In Maharashtra, TD Block officials work under the Zilla Parishad and Panchayat Samitis; the Tribal Welfare Officers work under the Tribal Welfare Department of the State Tribal Commissionerate, the Maharashtra State Cooperative Tribal Development Corporation through its own Regional and Taluk managers, and the Project Officers (of the rank of Deputy Collector) one each for an ITDP area, under the Collector who is Deputy Commissioner (Tribal) for sub-Plan schemes. The Chief Executive Officer of the Zilla Parished is the Assistant Commissioner. At Block level, the old set-up continues and the new set-up of the Growth Centre, Ashram School Complex and Adivasi Cooperative Society (ACS) has not come in force in its totality except for Ashram Schools and the ACSs which have been started under the general supervision of the Project Officer and organizational control of the District Deputy Registrar for Adivasi cooperatives, who functions under the Cooperative Department. All this has led to the unnecessary duplication of efforts—with a significant lack of coordination and a waste of human and material resources without the envisaged benefits to the tribal population. The machinery outlined in the Tribal sub-Plan was promising. The Unified Command Approach and the idea of intensive area development could have produced good results. But the cooperation and coordination between the various service departments remained a utopia and the respective officers' "allegiance" and responsibility being divided – due to duality of control over them – they are reluctant to act and use their discretion. The Collector (who is Deputy Commissioner for Tribal Development under the Maharashtra set-up) and is ex-officio Member Secretary of the District Planning and Development Council is so overburdened with the multiplicity of responsibilities that effective supervision and control is not possible. In fact it is necessary to vest more powers in the Tribal Commissioner (on the lines on which these were given to the Commissioner for Rehabilitation) whose directive would get priority over the orders from the heads of the various development departments and would eliminate the necessity for departmental approvals, so far as work under the Tribal Sub-Plan is concerned. Similarly, a Special Officer of the rank of and with the powers equivalent to the Collector should be posted as Additional Collector or Deputy Commissioner (Tribal Development) who will supervise, coordinate and direct the activities of the Project Officers and link them with the Project-cum-Block Development Officers of the TD Blocks and with other Departments functioning in the area. He himself would receive directives from the Divisional Development Commissioner and the Tribal Commissioner.

Expansion of TSP Outlay

The Maharashtra State Government has been trying to raise the share of the TSP, so as to reach 9 per cent of the Plan outlay of the State. Figures in Table 5.3 show the trend.

During the Seventh Plan period 5,01,036 Tribal families have been economically assisted against the target of 3,87,937 families.

The Tribal Area Sub-Plan has also supplemented by the Government of India in the form of Special Central Assistance. Special Central Assistance received from the Government of India during the period 1980-81 to 1990-91 is shown in Table 5.4.

TABLE 5.3 : Review of the sixth and seventh plans: Outlays on Tribal sub-Plan.

Sixth Plan

(Rs. in crores)

Year	State Plan		TSP		% of Outlay to State Plan Outlay (Col. 4 to 2)	% of Expend-iture to State Plan Expend-iture (Col. 5 to 3)
	Outlay	Expend-iture	Outlay	Expendi-ture		
1	2	3	4	5	6	7
1980-81	882.90	906.46	45.38	45.82	5.14	5.05
1981-82	1063.10	11,10.47	55.66	63.50	5.24	5.72
1982-83	1322.17	1357.68#	63.01	70.90	4.77	5.22
1984-85	1500.00	1500.00	71.68	73.20	4.78	4.80
1985-86	1650.00	1650.00	77.54	82.64	4.70	5.01
Total	6418.17	6524.61	313.27	336.06	4.88	5.00

Excluding unspent balance of Rs. 266.74 lakhs.

Seventh Plan

Year	State Plan Outlay	State Plan Expenditure	TSP Outlay	TSP Expenditure	% of Outlay	% of Expenditure
1985-86	1451.08	1728.24	82.45	89.61	5.68	5.19
1986-87	1805.37	1963.77	113.50	111.48	6.29	5.68
1987-88	2024.52	2190.47	145.48	147.89	7.19	6.75
1988-89	2108.77	2432.55	170.04	179.36	8.06	7.37
1989-90	2355.97	2511.22	202.16	189.44	8.58	7.54
Total	9745.71*	10826.25	713.63	717.88	7.32	6.57

* Per cent of TSP outlay is against budgetable outlay of State Plan during the seventh plan.

Only, Annual Plans for 1990-91, 1991-92 were formulated. The Eighth Five Year Plan (1992-97) and the Annual Plan also provided for the share of Tribal Sub-Plan as per the details given below.

Annual Plan 1990-91

In the Annual Plan 1990-91, an outlay of Rs. 179.55 crores was earmarked for the TSP out of the total budgetable outlay of Rs. 2,306.60 crores. The percentage of TSP outlay to the total budgetable outlay was 7.78 per cent. During 1990-91 families were benefited under the individual and family oriented beneficiary programme.

TABLE 5.4 : Special Central Assistance for Tribal Sub-Plan

(Rs.in lakhs)

Year	Special Central Assistance Released by GOI	Expenditure Incurred from Special Central Assistance
1980-81	544.16	544.16
1981-82	578.67	578.67
1982-83	646.00	721.23
1983-84	758.75	758.75
1984-85	799.33	801.57
1985-86	950.69	950.69
1986-87	1072.00	940.04
1987-88	1358.00	1248.00
1988-89	1447.49	1429.97
1989-90	1438.00	1438.00
1990-91	1581.80	1581.80

Annual Plan 1991-92

An outlay of Rs. 200.73 crores has been earmarked for the Tribal Sub-Plan in the Annual Plan 1991-92, out of the total budgetable outlay of Rs 2556.74 crores. The percentage of TSP outlay to total budgetable outlay is 7.85.

Eighth-Five Year Plan (1992-97) and Annual Plan 1992-93

An outlay of Rs. 1291.55 crores has been proposed (6.41 per cent) for the Tribal Sub-Plan area out of the total State Plan of Rs. 2,0294.43 crores for the Eighth Five Year Plan. As regards Annual Plan 1992-93, an outlay of Rs. 226.56 crores has been earmarked for the TSP out of the total budgetable outlay of Rs 3,476.16 crores (6.62 per cent). Emphasis is proposed to be laid on the completion of incomplete works, development of roads in the inaccessible areas, provision of basic minimum facility regarding drinking water, health, nutrition, Ashram Shalas and irrigation depending upon the local conditions.

Latest Administrative Set-up for the TSP

A separate administrative department, namely, Tribal Development

Department, at Mantralaya level has been created with effect from May 2, 1983. The Secretary of the Department has been designated as Secretary and Tribal Development Commissioner. Since March 1994, the post of Tribal Development Commissioner has been separated with H.Qs. at Nasik. At the State level there is a Cabinet Sub-Committee for Tribal Sub-Plan, headed by the Chief Minister which oversees all matters relating to the TASP and its implementation. The Tribal Development Commissioner is being assisted by two Additional Tribal Development Commissioners with headquarters at Nasik and Nagpur, respectively. Posts of 'Special Project Officer and Additional Collector' have been created for special tribal areas.

(i) The Division Commissioners of the Revenue Division of the State are fully responsible for the implementation of the Tribal Area Sub-Plan in their respecitve charges;

(ii) At the district level, the Collectors of Districts and the Chief Executive Officers of Zilla Parishads have been designated as Deputy Tribal Commissioners. The Deputy Tribal Commissioners are assisted in the district by Project Officers, who are full-time Class I officers. There are at present 19 Project Officers who are responsible for co-ordinating the functions of various departments.* They are entrusted with the work of preparing the project report, planning and monitoring the schemes, at the project level. The Block Development Officers and Assistant Registrars of Co-operative Societies in the Tribal Sub-Plan Area have been declared as Assistant Project Officers. The Government has also decided to place the services of the Tribal Welfare Officers under the supervision and control of the Project Officers;

(iii) There is a separate Directorate of Tribal Welface to deal with problems pertaining to the tribals. The directorate looks after Government hostels for Scheduled Tribe boys and girls, Ashram Shala Complexes, Ashram Shalas and Post-Basic Ashram Shalas run by Voluntery Agencies, supply of electric pump sets and oil engines, etc., to Adivasi Cultivators. The Project Officers of Integrated Tribal Development Projects are

* In eleven areas having large tribal population, Special Project Officers of the rank of Additional Collectors with near autonomous powers have been appointed.

ex-officio Deputy Directors. The Tribal Development Officers are now posted as Asstt. Project Officer under the Project Officers. (See the Flow Chart)

(iv) In order to ensure public participation in the implementation of the Tribal Area Sub-Plan, Special Executive Committees have been constituted under the District Planning and Development Councils of the 14 Tribal Districts, with following composition.

(1)	The designated Minister of the District (Palak Mantri)	Chairman
(2)	The Divisional Commissioner	Joint Chairman
(3)	One of the Tribal Elected Representatives (vide Serial No. 6 & 7 and if no tribal person is available, one amongst at Serial No. 9)	Vice-Chairman
(4)	Additional Tribal Commissioner (Tribal Development)	Vice-Chairman
(5)	President of the Zilla Parishad	Member
(6)	All Tribal MLAs/MLCs and MPs from the District	Members
(7)	Chairman of the Social Welfare Committee of the Zilla Parishad	Members
(8)	All Chairmen of the Panchayat Samitis falling in the area of operation	Members
(9)	Chairman of Zilla Parishad Works Committee	Member
(10)	Two Non-Official Representatives of the Tribal Districts	Members
(11)	One Adivasi lady member of the non-official members of DPDC.	Members
(12)	Chief Executive Officers of the Zilla Parishads	Members
(13)	Collector of the District	Member/ Secretary

The Administrative Departments are held responsible for executing the programme in the tribal area. They have been instructed to give special attention to tribal areas and to implement the programme effectively.

The Tribal Area Sub-Plan is also one of the items under the 20-Points Programme. The Programme is also being reviewed by the Committee specifically formulated for the review of the 20-Point Programme.

Protective Measures

The Government has enacted the following legislations in order to prevent the exploitation of tribals due to malpractices like land allienation, money-lending by money-lenders or traders at a higher rate of interest in the Tribal Sub-Plan areas:

(i) The Maharashtra Land Revenue Code Tenancy Laws (Amendment) Act, XXXV of 1974, which provides for –
   (a) Restoration to the original Adivasi owners (Tribal) of all their lands which have gone into the hands of non-tribals prior to the July 6, 1974, as a result of illegal transactions, i.e. transaction affected in Contravention of the law for the time being in force, and
   (b) Imposing stricter reservation on transfer of land from tribal to non-tribal after July 6, 1974 and providing for summary action by the Collector in case of breach.

(ii) The Maharashtra Restoration of Lands to the Scheduled Tribes Act (XIV of 1975) which provides for restoration to the original Scheduled Tribes owners of all their lands which have gone into the hands of non-tribals between the period from April, 1957, to the July, 1974, as a result of validly effected transfers including exchanges;

(iii) The Maharashtra Tribals Economic Condition (Improvement) Act, 1976, which prohibits money-lending to Tribals by money-lenders and trading in specified commodities by money-lenders and trading in specified commodities by private traders;

(iv) The Debt Relief Act, 1975 (Mah. III of 1976), which gives relief by liquidating the outstanding loans and interest payable of certain specified categories of persons which cover most of the tribals;

(v) The Maharashtra Sale of Trees by Occupants belonging to Scheduled Tribes (Regulations) Act, 1969, which provides restrictions for sale of any tree on holdings of Scheduled Tribes and also prescribes procedure for sale of trees after the Act came into force.

(vi) The Maharashtra State Tribal Development Corporation which was established in 1972 conducts the following activities:

   (a) Purchase and sale of agricultural and forest produce in the Tribal Sub-Plan areas as an agent of the Government under the provision of the Maharashtra Tribal Economic Condition (Improvement) Act, 1976.
   (b) Acts as an agents of the Government or any other Public Undertaking/Corporation in the Tribal areas and executes programmes entrusted by the Government.
   (c) Acts as a wholesale or retail distributor of articles, like foodgrains, cloth, etc. for the affiliated Adivasi Cooperative Societies (LAMPS) or on its own by opening retail outlets. The TDC has been entrusted with the monopoly procurement of foodgrains, grass, etc.

Special Action Plan for Selected Tribal Areas

Though the Tribal Sub-Plan is being implemented in the State for the development of tribal areas since the Fifth Five Year Plan, it was observed that certain inaccessible tribal areas with dense forests have remained undeveloped all along. It was, therefore, felt necessary to initiate special measures for ensuring speedy socio-economic development of these areas.

Special Action Programme, therefore, for Gadchiroli and parts of Chandrapur and Dhule districts were formulated in the year, 1989, with the objective of ensuring centain minimum developments of these areas within a definite time frame. In the SAP, emphasis has been laid on providing better facilities for communication (through road network), electrification, education, health, employment, irrigation, nutrition, etc.

Encouraged by the progress made under the SAP of the abovementioned districts, the Government sanctioned similar programmes for the extremely backward tribal taluka of Kinwat in

Nanded district and parts of Yeotmal district in April, 1990, and July, 1991, respectively. Funding pattern, relaxation of norms, etc., will be the same as for the SAPs for the district of Gadchiroli, Chandrapur and Dhule.

The broad outline of these programmes, their estimated cost expenditure during 1989-91, provision for 1991-92 (including additional funds) are shown in Table 5.5

TABLE 5.5: Estimated cost expenditure during 1989-91 provision for 1991-92

(Rs. in lakhs)

	District and Area	Total Estimated Cost	Period of Implementation	Actual Total Expen. during 1989-92 (Expenditure from Additional Outlay)	Total Provision for 1991-92	Additional Outlay Provided for 1991-92
	1	2	3	4	5	6
1	Gadchiroli (Entire District)	13430.00	3 to 4 years from 1989-90	4839.27	3035.19	1247.00
2.	Chandrapur (Entire) Rajura and Gond Talukas and parts of Mul and Chandrapur Talukas)	6104.00	3 to 4 years from 1989-90	1437.59	1026.99	531.00
3.	Dhule (Dhadgaon Taluka and part of Akkalkuwa Taluka)	1238.22	3 years from 1989-90	269.58	391.70	273.00
4.	Nanded (Kinwat Taluka)	1225.82	4 years from 1990-91	216.60	440.34	272.00
5.	Yeotmal (In Revenue 11 Circles in 7 Taluka)	2932.00	4 years from 1991-92	–	–	

A proposal for sanctioning Special Action Programme for parts of Bhandara district is under the active consideration of the Government.

These programmes are to be funded primarily from the normal provisions available for the District like that of outlays under District Plan, backlog, State Pool and nucleus budget Additional funds however, will be made available wherever necessary for the successful completion of these programmes. The Government has also relaxed the norms wherever necessary in order to ensure the benefits to the backward people of these areas.

Actual flow to the TSP during the Seventh Five Year Plan 1985-90 and Annual Plan, 1990-91, approved flow during 1991-92 and proposed flow for the Eighth Five Year Plan 1992-97 and Annual Plan 1992-93 are as indicated in Table 5.6.

TABLE 5.6 : Acutal Flow to the TSP during 1985-90 and 1990-93

(Rs. in lakhs)

		Seventh Plan Actual Expend-iture 1985-90	Annual Plan 1990-91 Actual Expendi-ture	Approved outlay 1991-92	Proposed Outlay	
					1992-93	1993-94
1.	Total State	1104450.00	252091.91	300000.00	347616.60	2029443.56
2.	Flow to TSP	69750.89	16282.41 (anticip-ated)	20086.10	22656.09	129155.77
3.	Percent-age	6.31	6.45	6.70	6.62	6.41

Special Action Plan-Reaction to Growing Terrorism

Though the Special Action Plan is a laudable step in accelerating the pace of development in remote inaccessible tribal areas, it has been criticized as basically a reaction to the growing terrorist activities in these areas. Incidentally Gadchiroli district and parts of Chandrapur district have been the strongholds of the Nascalite activities. Later the movement spread to the Kinwat area. Deori and other areas of Bhandara district have also shown increasing Naxalite activities. Thousands of State Reserve Police contingents could not completely control the growing Naxalite problem. Hence some top officers as well as leaders realized that unless development programmes were fully and properly implemented, mere gunpower would not be sufficient to control terrorism. So, to gear up the pace and qualitative aspects of development, this Special Action Plan was conceived and adopted. Whatever may be the reasons prompting this programme it will speed up development of these tribal areas.

Towards a Better Integration of Powers

In October 1993 the Chief Minister of Maharashtra disclosed a new decision taken by the Maharashtra cabinet according to which near autonomous powers would be vested in officials of the rank of Additional Collectors to oversee development of the backward tribal areas of the state. He said, the scheme will be operational in eleven areas of the state including Thane, Dahanu, Nasik, Kalwan, Melghat, Taloda, Nanded, Amavavali, Chandrapur and Gadchiroli, which have large tribal population.

The officials heading the scheme designated as Special Project Officer & Additional Collector' have been vested with complete administrative responsibility in the areas and will authorise development works such as the establishment of schools, hospitals, roads, agriculture, irrigation, hospitals, and drinking water supply, employment exchanges etc without requiring further sanctions from either the state secretariat or the district administration.*

The cabinet also decided to give additional allowances to officers at a cost of Rs. 14.70 crores as an incentive to enable the officers to maintain dual establishments if necessary since it would be mandatory for them to be physically present all the time in their area of operation as many of the tragedies in tribel areas like malnutrition etc are largely because the officials are absent in the areas and are not overseeing development schems personally. Hence forth the officials will reside at the block levels and it would be necessary for them to make themselves conversent with the local tribal dialect to ensure better coordination of the development schemes.

---

* Similar suggestions were made in author's book *Tribal Development Plans*' (1992), Concept Publishing Company, New Delhi, pp 152-55

Flow Chart

The Administrative Organization for the Tribal Sub-Plan in Maharashtra
(effective May 1, 1983)

Tribal Development Department

State Level Cabinet Sub-committe
heading by Chief Minister

(Mantralaya Level)

Secretary, TDD and Tribal Commissioner*
(Head of the Department)

Directorate of Tribal
Development
Director

Deputy Director
(Div. Level)

Tribal Dev. Officer
(T.D.O.)
(Recently placed as
Asstt. Project Officer
under the Project
Officer)

– Inspectors officer staff
– Ashram School Heads
– Hostel Chiefs

M.S. Coopve. Tribal
Dev. Corporation
Managing Director

Regional Managers
Taluka Managers

Additional Commissioner
(Tribal Dev.) at Nasik &
Nagpur (Divisional Level)

Dy. Commr. (T.D.) – Collector of
the Special Project Officer & Addnl.
Collector** District (District level)

Addnl. Dy. Commr. (T.D.)
– Chief Exevcutive Officer of
Zilla Parished (at Zilla
Parished Level)

Project Officer (ITDP)
(Project Level) of the Rank
of Dy. Collector in Class I

Asstt. Project officer 1
Research asstt. 1
Stenographer 1
Accountant/Headclerk 1
Driver 1
Peon 1

State Level Cabinet
Sub-committe heading
by Chief Minister

* Head Quarters at Nasik

** Since March 1994, separate Tribal Commissioner has been appointed with H.Qs. at Nasik.

6

PROBLEMS OF TRIBAL PEOPLE

TRADITIONALLY most of the tribal communities in India are agriculturist. After hunting and cattle-farming, agriculture was the third occupation which was followed and presently, with very little of hunting and decline in cattle-farming, agriculture is the main source of livelihood. But many tribals still practise primitive agriculture. In forests and on slopes of mountains and hills they practise shifting cultivation known as *Zoom* or *Penda* or *Dahiya* in different regions. In this mothod forest trees are cut in clusters over a place of land and allowed to dry and them burnt during summer. After a good rain the ashes get mixed with soil, and after this the tribals "broadcast" seeds (they don't plough or sow), that is, the seeds are thrown over the area. Usually the crops are of rice or minor millets like *Kodo* or *Kutki,* etc. They get good crops for two or three years and the output is good compared to the inputs of labour involved. After two or three years, they shift to some adjacent area and practise the same thing. This goes on for 10-15 years after which they return to the same original spot, thus completing a cycle. Though the Government has had schemes for stopping this method and settling the tribals on the plains giving them land, huts, cattle, agricultural inputs, etc., the practice has not been fully stopped though it is controlled. Some tribals who are rehabilitated on the plains again revert back to *Zoom* during the drought period or in calamities. A constant vigil, follow-up and alternative schemes to support their lives are essential. The wanton felling of trees also involves loss to economy. Among those tribals who are still living on mountains this practice is still in vogue in Assam, Bihar, Madhya Pradesh and even in Maharashtra. The author had occasion to witness the shifting cultivation in M.P. (among the Hill Korwas) and in Maharashtra (among the Madia

Gonds) during the eighties. At the beginning of the Seventh Plan, 8.5 lakh shifting cultivator families were identified. There were also 5,000 forest villages, which had their own problems.

Many tribals have adopted the traditional methods of cultivation and bullock pairs and iron plough have come to stay. However, they face many problems like irrigation, agricultural in-puts, e.g. seeds, manures, etc. Like any other farmer in India it is a gamble in rains. Due to a very low economic status, he faces hardships if the rains are untimely or insufficient. Though the development schemes have been implemented, the benefits either do not reach the tribals in remote areas or do not reach in time. Similarly as tribals are not accustomed to save and their staying capacity is low, the hardships faced are more severe than faced by other rural populations.

Land Alienation

In some tribal areas tribal farmers had small land holdings ranging between two and five or at the most 10 acres. A few had larger holdings. Unscrupulous money-lenders and traders grabbed and misappropriated their lands and either made them landless or labourers on their lands. *Malguzars* and *Zamindars*, even from their own community, who had power, inflicted hardships on them. Thus the tribals who were traditional farmers were turned into farm labourers and at times into bonded labourers. Later, though legislation followed declaring all transfers of land from tribals to non-tribals illegal, whether for a consideration or otherwise, the loop-holes were skilfully manipulated by the rich, defeating the very purpose of legislation.

Landless tribals who had their habitat in forests often encroached upon patches of cultivable land available in the forest in the vicinity of their villages. As a part of its social policy, the Government declared that all such encroachments in which FIR's had been filed would be regularized and *pattas* (rights in land) issued. But the Forest Department delayed and even failed in producing the encroachment warrants and so the tribals could not get the benefit. A more important snag in the policy was the non-settlement of forest land between the forest and the Revenue Departments due to which encroachment on many lands could not be settled. The result was continuation of the alienation of land and many tribals remained landless.

Forest and the Tribals

Most of the tribal communities have had their traditional habitat in forests. Forest had been their *home* since times immemorial and they had been the real forest guards before this function was taken over by *Zamindars* and later by the Government. Their exploitation of forest resources was for "use" and for subsistence and not for commercial purpose or for multiplication of wealth. Right from the British regime their traditional rights called *Nistar* rights were recognied by the Government. They could cut fire-wood and collect "minor forest produce". In its anxiety to preserve forests, the Government started making the forest laws stringent and restricted the rights of the tribals conveniently foregetting that much of the forest wealth had been destroyed by unscrupulous forest contractors who had an unholy nexus with some forest officers. As a result of the overenthusiastic, unrealistic policies of the Government (irrespective of its pious objectives), the tribal was rendered an "outsider" in his own traditional home – the forest. He became completely dependent on the forest officials, particularly the forest guards, foresters, etc., and was again exploited. The policy did not result so much in preserving the forest wealth but added a premium to the illegal gratification, which the tribals had to pay even for satisfying their genuine, primary needs such as fuel and fodder. However, it is heartening to note that though late, i.e. after sacrificing much in material and human values, wisdom has dawned on the Government, and now the Forest Department has started rethinking – even entrusting forest management to "tribals in the area/villages in a phased programme.[1]

Economic Exploitation

Economic exploitation of the tribal population has been going on since the British regime. Money-lenders, traders, roving merchants, etc., used to exploit him. When salt was not available in many tribal areas, it was sold in barter, weight to weight with paddy and even with *Chironji* (*Charoli*). Grigson and others have given examples of the exploitation by money-lenders. This dimension has been curbed but not fully eliminated as the new public banking system did not provide loans for unproductive purposes or for occasions like ceremonies, etc. Similarly the system lacks flexibility and is cumbersome and inconvenient for tribals. Hence they have to turn back to the traditional money-lender whom he considers close at hand, more sympathetic and personalized as against an unsympathetic bureaucrat of the bank/office. This again places opportunities to exploit in the hands of the traditional *Sahukar*.

The offices and officers at the grassroot or contact level who are supposed to reach them the economic benefits – whether in cash or kind, through loans, subsidies, things or services – have also created a bad record and bad impression on the tribal mind. They expect and accept bribes, share the benefits, delay the flow either due to the omnipresent red tape or wilfully and very little reaches the tribals.

A document published by the Government of India, in the Ministry of Home Affairs (1977) states[2] :

> "In the name of tribal development we have spent a lot of money during the last several Plans but when accounting was made at the end of the last period of the safeguards to the tribal in the Constitution, it was found that actual benefits trickling down to the tribals have not been consistent with the promise we have made. Expenditure has not resulted in the benefits that should have accrued to this population. Unfortunately, the development programmes for tribal areas did not yield the desired results"...
>
> More than 75 per cent of the total benefits have not reached the tribals. In the animal husbandry sector lot of money has been spent in the name of tribals and the benefits never reached them. The document laments, "we cannot have development at this rate."

Thus the development administration has added a new dimension to tribal exploitation. Those who are sent to ameliorate their poverty and misery join the bandwagon of exploiters, at times joining hands with the traditional exploiters, such as *Patwaris*, forest guards and foresters, rangers, some village-level workers, managers of Adivasi Co-operative Societies and many other petty officers including police constables, who have given rise to a new class creating more complicated problems. This has made the ground fertile for the activities of terrorists in the areas.

Social and cultural exploitation is also rampant. Tribal women/girls are victims of this exploitation. Tribal culture is misconceived. Their traditional dress and free behaviour is wrongly conceived. The outsiders such as contractors, truck drivers, government employees, etc., belittle their culture and consider it cheap and vulnerable. Girls are lured or enticed and fall victim to alurements. In some areas damage to the honesty and integrity of tribal men and women is to such an extent that they run after money and are ready to earn it by any means. This is a casuality attributable to the social cost of development. Their traditional arts, crafts, skills and nobility of mind are disappearing. Bad things are extended more easily and effectively by the agents of development than good and healthy ones. Social workers often say that a tribal village is considered as "developed" if the inhabitants have become dishonest, politicized (in a bad sense) and have started practising deceit. These negative fallouts of development are doing irreparable damage to the rich and classical fibre of the tribal culture.

"Dowry" is replacing "bride-price", and country liquor is replacing traditional *Toddy* and *Mahua* with increasing consumption as against the moderate one during the past.

Tribal Unemployment

Prior to administrative intervention, tribal economy was self-supporting subsistence economy and the tribal people were complacent, could satisfy their meagre wants and mainly depended on hunting, food-gathering, picking up of minor forest produce, primitive or traditional methods of cultivation wherein they worked on their own land and had some cattle, etc. With development, rights in forest were reduced, hunting, picking of forest produce controlled and during past years land was also alienated thus rendering many tribals landless labourers. They had to work as wage-earners under forest contractors or building contractors either in their own area or as migrants to other areas. Bonded labour also became common. This reduced them to such a low social and economic status as they had never experienced. Unemployment increased because those who never depended upon others for their livelihood were reduced to a dependent status. A few in the primitive areas reverted to shifting cultivation while some left the forest habitat and shifted to urban areas for jobs and became slum-dwellers facing all the miseries and agonies of the urban poor. Keeping the above in view creation of employment opportunities in or around their habitat is essential. Self-employment schemes, creation of new skills and supply of resources for setting up production units, cottage and small-scale industries based on local and farm or forest produce, giving training in forest management and entrusting the conservation and spread of forests to the tribals, etc., can help in solving the problems of unemployment or underemployment of the tribal population. This will also avoid unwilling and forced migration of tribal men and women which gives birth to cultural and psychological problems. This will also reduce the probabilities of bonded labour. Facilities and support to tribal handicrafts and their marketing in big cities through RMCs (Rural Marketing Centres) or Producers' Cooperatives will also help solve their problems and assist the growth of tribal economy. However, all middlemen and politics must be eschewed. Games and sports and cultural activities such as dancing, etc., also offer good avenues for providing the tribals opportunities to display their potentialities before the world. Limbaram's achievements at the international, pre-Olympic archery competitions in Sri Lanka (June, 1992) is a good example. Jiva Soma Masey, a *Warli* tribal, has demonstrated his drawing, painting talent even in foreign countries.

The development departments have planned and implemented some really imaginative schemes under the ITDP which clicked very well. To quote a few, the Animal Husbandry Department established training centres in the heart of the primitive tribal area (Bhamragad in Gadchiroli district of Maharashtra) and trained tribal youths in rearing of cows for three months, with a stipend. On completion of training, each youth was given a cow and a calf, and one bull for the village, and feed for six months. As a follow-up the Project Officer gave milk cans and bicycles thus converting the unemployed youths into milkmen. Piggery, poultry, fisheries and such other schemes with loans, technical know-how, etc., were successfully operated. It is essential to increase such schemes, with good follow-up, marketing facilities and a periodical review.

It has also been suggested that many items given to tribals under these schemes can be produced in the tribal areas with tribal labour, based on local resources and distributed through the agency of tribal people. This will reduce the costs, eliminate dependence on outside agency, assure timely supply and above all reduce scope for corruption.[3]

Problem of Education

Illiteracy and ignorance are the main hurdles in any programme of tribal development. In most of the tribal areas percentage of adult literacy after independance, ranged between zero and five per cent. Of late it has improved, particularly in the case of men, but the percentage of tribal literacy is still too low. (Table 6.1)

TABLE 6.1: Percentage of literacy among tribal populations

(Percentages)

Census Year	Rest of the Population		Scheduled Tribe Population
1961	Male	27.86	8.53
	Female	16.59	3.16
1971	Male	33.80	11.30
	Female	17.11	4.85
1981	Male	41.22	16.35
	Female	29.51	8.04

The National Adult Education Programme launched by the Government concentrated on three aspects, viz. functional literacy, functionality and awareness. Adult Education Centres were started in tribal areas and huge funds spent. The improvement in literacy percentage shown in Table 6.1 may be attributed to these efforts, though these figures, like many other statistical data, may not be fully reliable.

Primary education was also given to tribal children though primary schools, run by Zilla Parishads or Ashram Schools run by the Tribal Development Department. Initially, the response of tribal parents was poor, but when the students started coming, the government machinery proved quite inadequate. School buildings were not available at all places and teachers were also insufficient. Only one teacher taught two to four classes and at times in one room. Later two teachers were appointed in some schools. The teachers were reluctant to stay in tribal areas and mostly remained out of the headquarters. They did not know the tribal dialect nor did they know their culture. In the Ashram Schools which were up to middle school or rarely upto high school level children were sent because they were given free accommodation, food and even uniforms. The medium of instruction which was often the regional language was rather difficult for the children to follow.

Later, things improved as the Government decided to teach at least up to the second standard through the dialect of the children. Books were prepared and teachers given training in the tribal dialect and culture. As a policy, educated youths from the tribe or from the area who know their dialect were appointed. But there was another problem, that of the syllabi which were identical to those in that urban areas. The content of the courses had no appeal for the tribal students or their parents as the cultural content was different. Besides the content was considered useless as it did not help add to the livelihood of tribal population. Non-formal education which could improve the earning capacity of the tribals was essential. This component was also incorporated but on a meagre and experimental scale. Hostels were also started for tribal students in tribal areas. Some voluntary organiations – many run by tribal leaders – traditional or others – also started such schools and hostels. During the past two decades even colleges have been started in tribal areas.

This all has bad some good effect. Now there is god response to education from the tribal youths and their parents and "first learners" from many families are now "parents" themselves who do realize the importance of education. The problem now is of providing adequate and good educational facilities and to impart such education as would not just create armies of educated tribal youths like those urban/rural areas. Vocational education and facilities for self-employment should be provided. Those who show talent should be given enery support to acquire the highest qualifications and find good jobs. Care must be taken to see that the vigour and strength which characterize the tribal youths is not watered down by the educational process. The tribal youth should not aspire to be a white-collared wage-slave like others in urban area. Unwanted exodus to urban areas should also be discouraged and opportunities for employment provided near their home villages/towns.

Problems in Tribal Development[4]

The Integrated Area Development Approach was an imaginative step indicating understanding and comprehension of the tribal situation and the ITDP was a concrete programme for solving the tribal problems. In Maharashtra State alone 19 ITDPs were created,

10 in Sahyadri and nine in the Gondwana region. A special primitive tribes project was created at Bhamragad in Gadchiroli district. In addition to the schemes which were already being implemented through the subject matter departments. Special Central Assistance Schemes were also taken up in the essentially backward areas. This assistance was specially given by the Central Government for implementing schemes of local importance over and above the usual TSP funds.

A peculiar budgetary device under the TSP pattern was the provision for "nucleus budget". This fund was kept at the disposal of Project Officers of the ITDPs in order to draw up schemes of local applicability which were not included under the TSP budget. For long, planners have been criticied for unimaginative schemes, irrelevant to the local needs of the tribal population. Here a realistic solution was provided by the planners entrusting the micro-level planning to Project Officer on the spot.

The Directorate of Tribal Welfare functioned through Tribal Development Officers catering to the same tribal population with a different bunch of schemes. The State Tribal Development Corporations were created to induct business efficiency along with public accountability and were given autonomy for their economic pursuits. Many schemes continued to be implemented through the Project-cum-Block Development Officers of the TD Blocks which are still functioning in the TSP areas. Thus, three agencies for tribal development functioned in the same area with ultimate control in the same officer viz. Tribal Commissioner and Secretary, TDD of the State Government. Crores of rupees were spent since 1975 on the socio-economic development of tribals. In Maharashtra, 47.48 per cent of the total tribal population was covered under the TSP by 1987, the actual tribal population covered being 27.58 lakhs.

The evaluations occasionally made by different agencies and individuals do not present a very encouraging picture though not a gloomy one. Without going into the details of the total situation, let us ponder over the hurdles at the implementation level. It has been stated above that the planning was good and on the whole the schemes also were properly planned, keeping in view the socio-economic problems. Correctives to unrealistic planning also came up through the devices like the "nucleus budget" schemes. Even then, the tribal populations did not get the benefits as envisaged. The obstacles may be broadly classified as under:

(a) Problems with the administrative organisation;
(b) Problems of the socio-cultural level of the target populations; and
(c) The level of political awareness and leadership in the target groups.

(a) Problems with the Administrative Organization

Different agencies working for the same purpose in the same area functioned almost in an autonomus manner and the much talked of "integration" remained only on paper. Even under the TSP pattern, except the Additional Commissioner (Tribal Development at the divisional level) and Project Officer at the project level, all others (e.g. the Collector, i.e. Deputy Commissioner for Tribal Development; CEO, i.e. Additional Deputy Commissioner) were too busy to look after the implementation. Lack of collaboration and co-ordination between the TDO, the PCBDO and the Project Officer was one of the main hurdles at the project level. The Adivasi Co-operative Societies placed administratively under the Project Officer were functionally under the Taluka or Regional Manager of MSTDC. The Project Officer was without sufficient staff and his office became only a statistical record office for keeping the record of schemes implemented by different agencies. Except the "nucleus budget" schemes, he had no control over any other scheme or its implementing agencies. A very interesting feature was the existence of overlapping of functions on the one hand and lack of co-ordination on the other. The Project Officer was not entrusted with the powers to supervise and control the functioning of other departments in the area. As a result, he remained just a spectator and record-keeper of the schemes. In the Maharashtra pattern, he was also not expected to look after the socio-cultural welfare of the tribals and check those who do harm to it. (This was one of his functions under the M.P. pattern). The PCBDO also had no co-ordination with the project office. The TDO who was concerned with the Ashram Schools, hostels and distribution of electric pumps and oil engines was one more island of authority. When the MSTD Corporation made supplies to the Ashram Schools/Hostels or to the ACS and made purchases through them, there should have been perfect co-ordination between the TDO and the Corporation, with overall supervision and control with the Project Officer. The same can be said about the PCBDO and other subject matter departments.

The post of the Project Officer and Assistant Project Officer were left unmanned for years together. Revenue officers were sent as Project Officers without suitable training in tribal culture and problems. This was against the basic concepts of development administration. Of late, in Maharashtra, a good beginning has been made by directly recruiting persons as Project Officers from amongst those possessing a Master of Social Work degree and prior experience of working in the tribal areas. In fact, it is essential to recruit persons with basic post-graduate qualifications in Anthropology, Sociology, Social Welfare, Tribal Development or Development Administration, etc. The additional qualifications should include experience of extension work or social work in tribal/rural areas and acquintance with tribal culture and problems through advance-level research or social service.

Training at a TRTI or Universities should precede recruitment. As has often been emphasized by this author, even the Deputy Commisioner (Tribal) should be an officer with the training and background described above, with the status and powers (even magisterial powers) of a Collector, but not Collector himself. This is extremely vital in view of the growing law and order and political problems facted by the Collector, in addition to his revenue functions. Such a "Deputy Commissioner" can then effectively co-ordinate and supervise the work of different agencies through Project Officers. The newly created post of Special Project Officer and Additional Collector for some tribal areas may prove helpful in solving the above problems. Some officers from Forest Department and a few IAS officers have been appointed on these posts.

The personnel and resources can then by properly used for reaching the benefits to the tribals on time. For explaining the exact role and powers which the author wants to envisage at the Deputy Commissioner's level, following illustration is given. Electrification in tribal areas is a priority scheme for which lines were laid, but for many months or years they could not be energized because, in the connecting of the new lines to the supply lines, forest trees intervened. The permission of the Forest Department prusing or cutting down the trees. Could not be obtained. As a result, the electric poles prusing or cutting down the trees erected were left inoperative, some material was stolen or damaged and the benefits of development based on electricity did not reach the tribals. In some cases because of the non-settlement of land between the Revenue and Forest departments, technical difficulties also cropped up. The expenditure on the laying of electric lines thus remained unproductive for years. In such cases the Deputy Commissioner (Tribal) should be able to act and if he is convinced about the project and gives his approval (or on his recommendation the Additional Commissioners (Tribal) gives clearance the work should proceed presuming the consent of other Departments. Such overriding powers and authority only can effect real integrated development and assured co-ordination. Unless some such drastic breakthrough is accepted the socio-economic development of tribals may always remain in the doldrums. The Project Officer also should act as a powerful and effective authority under the Commissioner, rather than merely be a book-keeping authority for the roofing tiles distributed or bullock-carts given, etc.

(b) Problems of Socio-cultural Level of the Target Populations

Irrespective of the fact that the tribal populations were classified into primitive tribal groups and other groups, the level of acculturation is not something which can be mathematically estimated. Even within the same tribal population within the same habitat, cultural variations are seen and the economic conditions also differ. Unless the implementing officers at the grassroot level study these and adjust the schemes or provide a feed-back to the planners, many good schemes are likely to prove failures. Hence a background study of the people before they occupy the posts and a close study of their reactions to various schemes is essential. If necessary, certain schemes may have to be withdrawn without making it a prestige issue. Ignorance, illiteracy, superstitions and tradition orientedness are often the factors which obstruct the acceptance of schemes. It is also not advisable either to oppose or suppress such attitudes. A skilful extension/social worker (a skill which such officers ought to possess) will slowly defuse such attitudes, first by winning over the confidence of the clientele and then by making them accept the new ideas and schemes. The schemes should be initially in tune with their socio-cultural level. With the growth of awareness, other schemes will also be accepted.

Spread of education through various awareness programmes, programmes raising the level of functionality and implanting new schemes and result demonstrations can help in bringing out the attitudinal changes which form the basis of real development. Tribal women and children have the potential for development and hence this group should attract more attention. Moreover, change in the attitude of one mother or housewife spreads the idea to the whole family and thus to the community. If the above practical suggestions, born out of years of experimentation in tribal areas are kept in mind many hurdles at this level can be eliminated.

(c) Level of Political Awareness and Leadership in the Target Groups

We have adopted the democratic methods, and development, in general, was promoted through the decentralied democracy at the District, Panchayat Samiti and Village levels. When the development machinery carries the benefits to the tribals, the tribal leaders at all the three levels were supposed to act both as guards and as catalysts for development. In areas where there was some political awareness among the tribals, and/or they had conscious political leadership, the development schemes could by properly implemented. Unfortunately in many tribal pockets there were no such political leaders among the tribals, and in some areas the traditional feudal leadership was not development oriented, or even opposed to development schemes. In some areas the leaders were non-tribals and many of them committed to ideologies exotic to the tribal culture and life. In the democratic bodies at the District and Panchayat Samiti levels, the members and office-bearers proved too shy and meek to control the development machinery and even to safeguard the interests of their brethren. A few educated individuals from the tribals, who had the capacity to lead, alienated themselves from the group. As a result, political leadership and political awareness among the masses remained dim. The schemes were either not properly implemented or the benefits were siphoned off resulting in pilferage of funds and corruption. Discontent grew in the areas clearing fertile grounds for unlawful activities, the terrorist groups complicating the whole situation. Development in the area, therefore, is not possible unless there is an attitudinal change which can come only through the consistent efforts of the tribal leadership.

In contrast to this the work of individual social workers and voluntary organiations in tribal areas is pioneering and a lot promising considering the constraints of human and monetary inputs. This model has to a large extent supplanted the tribal leadership. The need now is for a new line of local tribal leadership which is development oriented and constructively active for the welfare of their own community and areas.

Much has been done, but a lot more could have been done, had these hurdles been properly tackled. The beneficiary should feel that he is getting the needed benefit. Planning should be from below and implementation honest, fool-proof and timely. The machinery at the district level and below should be harmoniously synchronized to function as a cohesive unit. Unity of command at the district and divisional level with provisions for removing administrative bottlenecks is essential. Co-ordination between non-political voluntary organisations/workers will also be helpful. The traditional community spirit in the tribals should be utilised for development and the local tribal leaders (traditional or new) should be involved in the process. Last but not least is the shift in emphasis from the target-oriented concept of development to the change in attitudes of the tribals and a voluntary acceptance of the development schemes.

REFERENCES

1. Deogaonkar, S. G., 1992, *Tribal Development Plans*, Concept Publishing Co., New Delhi, p.160.
2. Government of India, "Approach to the Development in the sixth plan : A preliminry perspective", *Occasional Papers on Tribal Development No. 17*, Ministry of Home Affairs, New Delhi, 1977, pp. 90-100.
3. Deogaonkar, S. G., 1992, *Tribal Development Plans*, Concept Publishing Co., New Delhi, pp. 162 – 165.
4. Based on an article by the Author published in the Special issue of *Tribal Research Bulletin* on the theme, "Socio-cultural Dynamics of Tribal Life", of the Tribal Research and Training Institute, Government of Maharashtra, Pune, 1990.

7

THE PERSONNEL POLICY

ONE of the most importaut aspects of any administrative organization is the personnel policy. This assumes special significance when it is required for bringing about planned changes in a community. It is an establishzed principle that people first accept a person and then his ideas or acts. When the community development programme started it was emphasied by S.K. Dey and others that persons from the revenue set-up should not be inducted in the development machinery as they would try to apply the "revenue method", i.e. of coercion and compulsion. What was required was persuasion and a willing acceptance of the new idea by the beneficiaries. The early Block Development Officers were selected accordingly and trained properly to orient them to the requirements of the programme. When it came to tribal development, selection of personnel assumed more importance due to the typical socio-cultural conditions and the psychological set-up of the tribal mind. Apart from a knowledge and understanding of the tribal and the scenario, they required administrative skills, imaginativeness, courage, integrity of high order and the mental make-up of a social worker. The early workers in the field like Shri A.V. Thakkar (Thakkar Bappa), Dr. Verrier Elwin, and early administrators, like Prof. C. Von Furer Haimendorf, Shri L. M. Shrikant, academicians like Prof. Behram H. Mehta, followed by contemporary administrators like Dr. Brahma Deo Sharma and some others can be cited as examples.

Though the thinking on this aspect was proper and abundant, it could not be translated into action, and as a result, the State Governments who were entrusted with the actual handling of the programme appointed administrators of whom very few were suitable for the task. This was more true about officers appointed in the field, who were in actual contact with the people. They lacked the necessary qualities, background, and temperament and had no orientation. Going against the stipulated norm of community development, even revenue officers were posted. The Class II and III personnel were also sent without any practical consideration. The worst part was the practice of sending persons who had bad service records to tribal areas as punishment. Thus many inefficient, corrupt persons with addictions were sent to tribal areas. As a result, either they did not work, and very often remained away from the headquarters, or stayed in the area (keeping their families at distant towns/cities) and indulged in drinking, and exploited the tribals. Corruption became rampant. Such persons considered posting in a tribal area as the worst possible punishment and felt that nothing worse could happen to them. So they became hard nuts to crack. Such persons were not expected to do much, and the result was accordingly.

Paul Appleby had said in his report that recruitment to public services in India should be more aggressive and imaginative. This was more true for manning the posts in the tribal development administration. However, this was not done and, as a result, persons unsuitable for the posts were recruited and posted at different levels. What in fact should have been done was to get proper personnel through recruitment based on innovative methods like those adopted by private industries or voluntary social organizations. Posts should have been advertised and persons with right temperament, aptitude and enthusiasm recruited on a contract basis (if necessary). With proper training they should have been posted in tribal areas with proper facilities and incentives for god work. After the initial contract period, both the parties (the Government and the employee) could have decided about continuation of the contract. The author had occasion to see persons/youths with a sense of purpose who entered the service and worked with enthusiasm. But they were either transferred or left because of an uncongenial and bureaucratic atmosphere which was not conducive for persons who wanted to work. Bad money drives away good money. This is true in all spheres.

Even while transferring persons to tribal areas the best personnel should be selected. Because it is they who have to impress the tribals.with their attitude, behaviour, sincerity and integrity.

Proper facilities must be provided for them so that they are not tempted to remain out of the headquarters. For those who are married and have children studying in schools, colleges, etc., a family quarter should be provided in a city or town and the officer may be given a small two-room flat with facilities of a cook, etc., in the field. A few such officers may be housed in a small guest house with a cook and kitchen to be managed by the government. Those who work well and show results should not be kept too long in the area unless the officer himself is willing to continue. After a definite span (three-four years) he should be given a townposting and others posted to the tribal area. Another important aspect is rotation of officers of higher ranks between field and apex level. It is often observed that some officers at the Secretariat or Directorate level tend to lose contact with field. As a result they are unable to appreciate and weigh the assessment furnished by the field staff. Some officers from the field then tend to give an unrealistic assessment and point a rozy picture which flatters the headquarters but goes against the interest of a proper feed-back from the field. A code of conduct is also needed for officers working for the tribal development. Drinking and such other addictions must be banned. Exploitation of tribal men, women and teenagers in all forms by officers at all levels should be severely punished. There should be a strict vigil on corruption in any form.

Initial selection of officers may be based on the background of the needs of the programme. Qualifications in social sciences in general and in Anthropology, Sociology, Public Administration, Management, Social work, up to the post-graduate level in particular may be given preference. The University Grants Commission has been sponsoring different extension programmes through universities and colleges, like National Service Scheme (NSS), Adult Education, Mass Programme for Functional Literacy (MPFL), Jana Shikshan Nilayam (JSN), Continuing Education, etc. Students who work in such programmes develop some attitudes and get experience of working among the rural/tribal poor. Such students should be given preference. Persons with experience of working in voluntary organizations should be preferred. Those officers who have had no experience in such subject/field-work should be given some training organized at universities, colleges, and in organizations which are engaged in a similar type of work, both at theory and field levels.

Unless such criteria and techniques are adopted in letter and in spirit, a real breakthrough in the personnel policy will not come.

Unless the officers entrusted with development at all levels don't develop the personality and approach needed for the job, they cannot win the confidence of the people whose development is entrusted to them. The author had occasion to move through tribal areas with Prof. C. Von Furer Haimendorf, an anthropologist-administrator and could observe the way in which he tackled the tribal people and their problems. He squatted on the floor, talked in *Gondi* fluently, offered *bidis* or tobacco to them and ate things prepared by them. Where one young couple accompanying to see the area tried to pluck a guava fruit from a tribal's courtyard he discouraged them and said that the tribals often feel that outsiders came to take away things from them and if we pluck fruits, etc., their image (bad) about us would be confirmed. Give them things, don't carry away from them.

Similarly, the habit of asking the middleman or liaison to arrange dances of tribals for entertaining outsiders, officers, etc., is not fair; even if you pay *bakshis* for it. If you stay among them for a couple of days and do some good work, establish rapport, the tribal people would themselves offer to dance treating you as their guest; and express love, gratitude for you. All this is based on experience of working among tribals for the last many years and as such are not mere theoretical dogmas. The officers entrusted with development must entertain proper outlook to human relations and adjust their behaviour to the needs of the job.

Recruitment of tribal youths for manning posts in tribal development is basically a good idea. But one must know and remember that many tribal youths who are educated may go away physically and emotionally from their people thus alienating them psychologically from their own people. They are then not ready to stay among their own people. Such persons would do a great damage to development. It is a matter of experience that many persons from among the same community exploit their own people when entrusted with power – whether political or bureaucratic. Persons who may not be from the same tribe/community but have the proper aptitude and attitude for tribal development have done well at all levels, viz. as leaders, officers and social workers. However, if we get the right type of person from the same tribe/community he should be preferred because he would be accepted easily and quickly by the people.

While inaugurating the Development Commissioners' Conference on Community Project on May 7, 1952, Jawaharlal

Nehru said:[1]

> "I suppose there is hardly a country—and I speak with all deference to other countries—in the world which has such high ideals as India. And I may add that there is hardly a country where the gap between ideals and performance is so big as in India."
>
> Of course he was not against "gazing occasionally at stars", but being a pragmatist, he cautioned against the danger of talking very big and not going anywhere near the objective. Late Smt. Indira Gandhi had rightly retorted to the criticism by some leaders, who said that Pandit Nehru was a "dreamer", by saying that "only those who can dream can plan for the future".

Down-to-Earth Attitude

However, Nehru's realism and "down-to-earth" attitude on development are fully reflected when he says:

> "We have got into the habit of doling out good advice to everybody, to the country, to our people. Nevertheless, my experience has shown that people who give too much of advice are not liked. They irritate. If we function too much from the top without adequate foundations and without that intimate relation with the lower rungs and foundation itself, we can hardly achieve any great thing." He hurries to add, "Obviously it is necessary to plan, to direct, to organize and to coordinate, but it is even more necessary to create conditions when spontaneous growth from below is possible and can take place".[2]

Human Being the Primary Matter

Advocating a sense of intimate partnership between the administration and the people Jawaharlal Nehru says, "It is not good enough to sit in our chambers and decide everything according to what we consider is the good of the people . . . the people should be given an opportunity to affect our thinking." Verging on harshness he says, "the primary matter is the human being involved, the man who is going to work, to feel it and translate that feeling into action. Are you going to try to create that type of human being ? The human being is there of course; you have only to reach his heart and mind. Take it from me, do not advise so much, do the job yourself. Do it, and others will follow. Why do you think it is your business to sit in a big office because you are Development Commissioners and issue orders ? If I may say so with all respect, you are no good if you do that. Better go somewhere else and do some other job. Get clear about this."[3]

The type of administration and the administrators which he envisaged for bringing about development of our backward areas is very clear from the above excerpts from his speech.

Nehru's Views and Our Performance

With the background of Pandit Nehru's vision if we review our efforts for tribal development we find a mixed picture. One has to admit that much has been done and there have been changes in all tribal groups including the primitive groups who are at a very low level of acculturation. However, we also must accept our failures on many counts. In spite of different arganizational structures created for tribal development some problems have not been solved. Had Pandit Nehru been alive he would have been grieved and annoyed to see the following :

(1) Though the exploitation at the hands of traditional money-lenders or *Sahukars* has been largely checked, economic and social exploitation still continues in new forms and by new persons—tragically enough even by those who are entrusted with their protection and development.

(2) In spite of huge funds spent on the development of the tribal areas (the records speak of crores of rupees) roads and bridges are not visible in many areas, keeping them cut off from the outside world for three to eight months in a year.

(3) In spite of multiplicity of agencies for tribal development (to name a few, Project-cum-Block Development Officer, Project Officer-ITDP; Tribal Development Officers, Tribal Development Corporation, Forest Department – which is also entrusted with a few schemes, etc.) a lot of work remains to be done, and the beneficiary either does

not get the benefit, or does not get in full, or does not get in time. One of the reasons is the presence of such multiple agencies with overlapping of functions, lack of co-ordination and of the much talked of "integration".

Introspection

Men of Peculiar Timber Needed

Without going into numerous other points which could have pained Nehru (including the omnipresent demon of corruption) let us try to diagnose the points from Pandit Nehru's angle.

In a bureaucratic set-up of development, the officers entrusted with development must be persons of a peculiar timber – a timber which is at once democratic and aim-oriented. While talking about the Block Development Officer, Panditji had said,[4] ". . . the success will depend upon the *quality* (emphasis added) of the BDOs. They are or should be, 'the salt of the earth'. If we build up a high level, competent and enthusiastic body of BDOs all over the country, we would have provided the wherewithal for rapid progress. The BDO must, of course, have competence and enthusiasm. He must have *elan*".[5] Let us introspect ourselves. Do we have such personnel in our team ? If not, are we ready to change our methods of recruitment to the posts ? We have grown so frigid after Nehru that we just want to trod on.

People having experience of working with communities know that the people – more so the tribal people – first accept a person and then his programmes. It is *he* who brings about the attitudinal change through human factors. Pandit Nehru said, ". . . it is the training in the human approach which is not always easy. . . . how to put this spirit of excitement of doing things in the people ? . . . I look back to the Gandhian era. Gandhiji came into the field and . . . within a short space of time he electrified chiefly the countryside. He was a remarkable individual. We cannot compare with him."[6] Without formal training he could create confidence and change the rural masses, and, even his co-workers did the magic. Explaining the reason Pandit Nehru says, ". . . the people had faith in them, had faith in their integrity, in their honesty of purpose. . . . The fact remains that you can only deal with these people if you instil in them a certain hope and a certain faith and a certain belief in your integrity; otherwise your lessons will not go far."[7]

Can we assure ourselves that we possess these qualities ? Organisational restructuring and financial in-put can bring about development if the agents of development are persons visualized by Pandit Nehru. Presuming a positive role of bureaucracy in a Welfare State he advocated that "the gap that separates the official from the people must lessen and disappear . . . and it is in the measure that it disappears it succeeds in influencing the people".

A correct personnel policy is extremely important so far as the successful implementation of tribal development is concerned. Proper selection, adequate and suitable training and creating a sense of dedication in every worker in the administrative machinery are essential. High standards of integrity, morality and sincereity must be maintained. Only such persons who are amenable to this discipline may be sent to the area. The zeal, perseverence and tenacity of a social worker must be present. He must accept the job, not only as a challenge but as a mission which he promises to fulfil as a "man" and as an officer of the Government. Only such an attitude can keep the morale at a high level.

In fact it is better to leave the conclusion to every person who reads and ponders over the points which are put forth in the foregoing paragraphs. In spite of large investments and ambitious programmes, why is it that tribal development is not uniform and up to our expectations ? The tribal populations are now in a mood to accept the change. Naturally it is our responsibility, i.e. of the planners, administrators, social workers and those enlightened citizens who can feel the breeze of change to see that the forthcoming initiative is matched by timely and appropriate fulfilment of their demands. Apathy, lethargy, insincerity and corrupt practices must now come to an end. When awareness of their rights dawns in the tribal mind – and that is what we have been trying to develop – and they desire and demand better and fuller life (as against their traditional meagre wants) we must rise up to their expectations or else their awareness may take an undesirable turn disturbing not only the development scene but even peace and tranquillity. If we follow Panditji's advise his soul and we all will get peace.

REFERENCES

1. Govt. of India, 'Inaugural Address delivered by the Prime Minister at the Development Commissioners' Conference on Community Projects on 7th May, 1952, *Community Projects - A Draft Hand Book*, C.P.A. Planning Commission, 1954, New Delhi, p.3
2. Govt. of India *Ibid;* p. 1
3. Govt. of India *Ibid*; p. 4
4. Govt. of India, 'Message of the Prime Minister Jawaharlal Nehru', *National Conference on Community Development at Mysore City* (23rd. to 28th July 1959), Main Recommendations and Conclusions, Min. of C.D. Cooperation, Sept. 1959, New Delhi, p. 50
5. Govt. of India, *Ibid:*
6. Govt. of India, 'Adress by the Prime Minister, April 29, 1957' *Summary Records of Sixth Development Commissioners' Conference on Community Projects*, held at Mussoorie, (26-30 April 1957) Dec. 1957, New Delhi, pp. 62-63
7. Govt. of India, *Ibid*; p. 64

8

TRIBALS' RESPONSE AND CULTURE CHANGE

DR. VERRIER ELWIN headed a Committee "to study the working of the Special Multipurpose Tribal Block and to advise the Government of India on how to implement the intensive development programme of the Blocks more effectively and give the programme a proper tribal bias". The Committee recommended delimitation and allocation of Tribal Development Blocks with a "tribal touch" or tribal bias. Dr. Elwin described "tribal touch" as—

> "A 'tribal touch' or 'tribal bias' means that we must look, if we can, at things through tribal eyes and from the tribal point of view. We must find out what means most to them. We must see that they do in fact get a square deal; we must save them from the exploiters who still invade their villages, and ensure that in future they will be in a position to administer and develop their own areas."
>
> "A tribal bias means that we recognize and honour their way of doing things, not because it is old or picturesque but because it is theirs, and they have as much right to their own culture and religion as any one else in India. It means that we must talk their language, and not only the language that is expressed in words but the deeper language of the heart. It means we will not make the tribes ashamed of their past or force a sudden break with it, but that we will help them to build upon it and grow by a natural process of evolution. It does not mean a policy of mere preservation; it implies a constant development and change, a change that in time will bring unbelievable enrichment, as there is ever closer integration in the mainstream of Indian life and culture."

The tribals are a section of humanity, simple, tough and hardy, convinced of the wholesomeness of its own way of life. Their existence depended for centuries on forests and mountains, upon the challenges from nature and their response to it. Rigorous climate could not drive them away from their homelands nor obliged them to abandon their way of life. But then, Dr. Elwin observes, they do not suffer from the obstinacy of adherence to the beliefs. They are open and frank and willing to change when faith and reason convince them that a change is necessary. Thus, it depends upon the personnel, especially at the grassroot or contact level who are supposed to implement the development scheme to convince them. But before doing this, answers to two questions become important. Do the agents for development themselves believe in the efficacy of what they are canvassing and are they themselves convinced about it, and, secondly, by their sincerity of purpose and honesty, have they won over the confidence of the tribal people whom they are supposed to convince about the development schemes ?

Tribal Response to Government Schemes

While working for tribal development we are restructuring and changing a traditional society. Hence care ought to be taken of the acceptability and feasibility aspects of the programme. An analysis of the socio-cultural aspect of the local tribal community and its beliefs and practices will provide a background on which acceptability of a particular scheme would depend. Though it is presumed that the envisaged changes are meant to alter the traditional attitudes and behaviour, it is not advisable to try a total and sudden break with all traditions, lest they strongly resist any change or grow apathetic to the development programme. The changes on which getting their support is easy and immediate good results can be demonstrated should be introduced first, and others may be kept aside for the time being.

Experience shows that the tribals give positive response on certain items. These include cultural items like singing, dancing, games and sports, the communications including roads, bridges, bus transport, new avenues of employment like skilled or unskilled labour, imparting some skills like carpentry, pottery, brick-work, metal-work, and animal husbandry, piggery, poultry, fishery, and so on.

Similarly water-storage tanks/lakes, contour bunding, improved methods of agriculture, drinking water facilities such as wells, tube-wells, etc., evoke good response.

On the other side, changes in food habits, ending superstitions, use of modern allopathic medicine, sending children to schools, adult education, etc., do not evoke quick response. It is only after slow changes in attitudes take place that these aspects should be taken up. The role of the traditional leaders such as *Mukhiya*, *Patel*, some Chieftain or Maharaja is also important. If these leaders support development the tribal population will also accept it. However, experience shows that such chiefs try to preserve their traditional status, importance and privileges by opposing schemes for development. They feel that a better life, more awareness and education, self-sufficiency to tribals would mean a blow to their feudal leadership. Therefore, first such leaders should be "converted", and then the job would be easier.

New problems arise when the tribal population starts giving a positive and favourable response to developmental schemes. Then their demands for getting benefits increase and it is at this juncture that development administration falls short of providing the needed benefits. It has been observed in many tribal areas that when the tribals demand improved seeds and manure they don't get these on time and when they realize the importance of allopathic medicines, the State dispensaries either have no qualified doctors or lack medicines. When tribal parents realize the importance of sending children to schools, these are without proper class-rooms or have inadequate teachers and so on. Tribals used to eat raw vegetables, meat or in roasted form. We changed their habit to cooking of food, but now they don't get adequate fuel. Traditional *Sahukars* and traders are replaced by Banks or credit societies but these don't provide loans on time. Monopoly purchase schemes for paddy, *mahua* flowers and other minor forest produce were introduced but the cooperative societies or other facilities created for the purpose failed to function due to lack of funds or absence of concerned officers from the headquarters, etc. As a result the poor tribal who is still practising barter transactions was forced to go to private traders and sell his product at a throw away price. Red tape and corruption in the administration also discourage tribals from taking advantage of many good innovative schemes.

Many schemes implemented through ITDP, IRDP, etc., evoked

good response. But after a few years the tribals were discouraged due to bad experience. Certain schemes failed due to lack of proper follow-up by the concerned department or a sister department. Some examples are, supply of roofing tiles (Mangalore tiles), construction of gobar-gas plants, supply of oil engines or electric pumps for irrigation, etc. These schemes needed follow-up in the form of advice, maintenance, replacement, supply of secondary articles, e.g. diesel, etc. But this was not forthcoming. Due to this, schemes which could initially evoke a very good response, failed to make much headway.

The response of tribal people to various developmental schemes also varies from place to place, and also area-wise. Similarly it differs from tribe to tribe or even amongst sub-groups of a tribe. The socio-economic status of a family and the level of literacy are also significant as they affect the capacity to understand the importance of a scheme and its value for the family or community. A survey conducted to find out the response of tribals from Thane district in Maharashtra (1976) showed that[1] the level of literacy in a tribal family had direct correlation with the socio-economic status of a tribal family which had further correlation with the size of the family. The bigger the size of the family, the higher has been the socio-economic status and a high level of literacy in the family. This covered tribals from the *Katkaris* (small families and poverty stricken low economic status) among whom only 7 per cent were literates. Others like Kokna tribals had a higher economic status, large family sizes and the level of literacy among them was 49.5 per cent. The tribals felt that education up to standard VII for their wards was sufficient because, they believed, too much education resulted in alienating their children from land and farming.

Evaluatory studies indicate that the tribal populations have now been introduced to the schemes planned for their development and awareness regarding the new components canvassed therein has now been realised by them. But they are cautious while accepting these schemes for various reasons. They are doubtful about the end product and still have inhibitions about the ultimate utility of the schemes for their family/community. Apathetic attitude of officers, absence of follow-up of the schemes in many cases, red tape and corruption have all contributed to reinforcing their fears. When a traditional/conventional mode is discontinued the modern or non-conventional mode must succeed—or should be made to succeed—or else the tribal is let down from both sides.

Evaluatory studies of various schemes must be conducted on a large scale and in different areas to find out the drawbacks at the implementation stage. These can guide the planners and administrators at all levels in reviewing their schemes.

Tribal Culture and Development

The process of development inevitably affects culture. To Malinovski, culture represents a total way of life which secures for an individual the satisfaction of his bio-physical drives and the fulfilment of other wants and cravings and ultimately invests him with freedom. Radcliffe-Crown regards culture as cultivation, the process of handing down and acquiring traditions, as a result of which society is perpetuated. Herskovits defines culture as that part of a man's total setting which includes the material objects of human manufacture, techniques, social orientations, points of view, and sanctioned ends, which are the immediate conditioning factors underlying behaviour. Culture is handed over to each and every individual within a society or a group. Thus when a child or an individual learns to conform to his her own cultural tradition, we call the process as *enculturation*. When there is an exchange of culture traits and complexes, we call it *trans-culturation* and when one way of life is being displaced by anothyer, under the influence of another culture, the process is called *acculturation*. This may lead to assimilation. However, it is also likely that at a certain stage, the dominated culture breaks down at first and then recovers to develop a reaction to the loss of its own individuality. Such a reaction is called *contra-acculturation*. But this may not happen if some community exposed to other dominant culture around it is emotionally affected by them. Mental images of persons and objects are formed, and original ideas, and values are lost, and in their place new ideas, values, traits are slowly adopted. This process is then called *introjection*.

The process of development changes the ideas, values, traits, attitudes and behaviour. This manipulation is likely to create tensions and either apathy or even resistance from the community. Between generations (e.g. the old and the young) and between individuals, the responses can be different, giving rise to culture lag and discontent or frictions. Therefore, it is the responsibility of the planners as well as the implementing authorities to see that either such tensions are avoided or at least minimized. A sudden and thorough break with the cultural tradition or a sort of uprooting ought to be avoided. Many good things or even the less harmful traits from their tradition need not be disturbed. Even for introducing changes, mental images may first be influenced. Physical aspects, which may have a remote connection with some aspect of their culture, are easily traced. Such things must be identified first. For this purpose a good study and understanding of the tribal culture is necessary.

The socio-psychological processes are, consciously or sub-consciously, at work and precede cultural changes. In 1932 Thurnwald developed a theory of cultural change and its psychological causes and concomitants. On this basis cultural anthropologists developed the premise that the cultural change essentially depends upon the culturally institutionalized and individually internalized value imaginations. Such internalization of "exotic" values causes some break with the past. There is a loss of old values and a grappling with the "new" values. This affects attitudes and later the institutions. The tribal thus stands between the world of tradition which is being left behind and the world of progress which is being offered to them. It is here that the cultural and social anthropologist can play a catalytic role for development. The Xth ICAES (*International Congress of Anthropological and Ethnological Sciences*) held at New Delhi during 1978 (and presided over by late L.P. Vidyarthi) deliberated on the theme, "Anthropology and Development".

Role of Anthropology

Anthropology provides knowledge which can be used for pushing forth development. Study of political anthropology has enriched the knowledge and understanding of political processes in different communities in the world. Political science owes much to the contribution of anthropology. Similarly cultural and social anthropology can be of great help in bringing about desired changes in communities. As and when new ideas, values, norms of behaviour and material aspects are canvassed in tribal communities the initial reaction is either negative or apathetic as the things or ideas don't fit in their existing conceptual forms. The gap between culture gives rise to a cautious reaction. However if those who plan the schemes and implement them are conversent with the traditions, customs, norms, mythology and other aspects of their culture, they can identify such aspects from the package of development which can be correlated to the ideas/images obtained in their (tribal) culture. These can then be canvassed giving examples of similar things/ideas from their culture. However remote the correlation may be, it does influence the minds of people. Knowledge of their dialect and folk literature can also be very useful for winning their confidence and introducing new ideas. Their traditional performing arts such as singing, dancing, etc., can also be used for organizing them and augmenting the enthusism in their community. Tribal communities still have an organic community life with an egalitarian and socialist relationship within the community. This can be harnessed and developed on modern lines. Their traditional community institutions like youth dormitaries, village councils, elders' councils, panchayats, etc., can be used for developmental purposes, as their basis is a strong sense of organic unity of their community and not "politics". The elected statutory panchayats are no substitute for these traditional institutions. The election process is still new to the tribals as they often work on the basis of consensus which is a result of free thinking for the welfare of their community. Honesty, respect for authority and obedience to norms or rules accepted as the basis for the survival of their communtiy are the bases of their unity. If these institutions and processes are influenced properly and utilized for the purposes of development, the pace can be quickned. The change which breaks a tradition should not be sudden and the break too great. The pace should be slow. Similarly the agent of change should first convert a few progressive individuals from their community who can go ahead with the process. Women in tribal communities are better prone to change as compared to men, but knowledge of the dialect is more essential while communicating with women. Schemes for children and their mothers are better accepted and yield better results. Influencing the mind of a woman – a mother, a wife or a sister – has a multifold effect on the family.

The disciplines of sociology and anthropology can be of great help in solving problems of tribal populations. Dr. Wolfgang K. Knabe who was then at the University of Augsburg, Department of Sociology (erstwhile W. Germany) presented a paper based upon his field research experience, at a seminar organized at Amravati (Maharashtra) by the author for the Tribal Research and Development Council.[2] Basing his theoretical premises on the writings of sociologists from Fed. Rep. of Germany, notably Reimann, Horst, Haag, Fritz and others, Dr. Knabe suggested two starting points for handling the problems, viz. ethnomethodology and action-research strategy.

By participant observation, ethnomethodology seizes the subjective reality of experience of the tribal population from its every day relations. The essential traditional contents of culture are identified. Thus, ethnomethodology discovers the instrument which can be used for solving problems with action-research strategy. Knabe quotes Lewin who pioneered this strarting point, and described it as comparison of the effects of different forms of social handling and investigations of ways of behaviour and inter-group relations. The aim is to motivate the tribal people to take personal decisions. If this process continues, the anthropologist can decide on how to alter the behaviour and draw the expected response. The process continues till the desired socio-cultural change is guaranteed by the self-created recognition processes in the tribal community. Thus it is agreed that a static, ethnocentric culture-groups behaviour can be engineered by sociologists and anthropologists in such a manner that the groups behaviour will change and slowly turn to a dynamic culture responding to changing situations and guiding itself towards a new pattern of culture suitable to changing environment.

The use of culture for changing culture is possible and has been tried with good results. The agents of change must know which aspects of culture should be left untouched to start with and which aspects should be handled first. But, for this purpose, he must be conversant with those aspects and expressions of culture which are easily discernible. Tribal folk-lore is an important manifestation of tribal culture and way of life.

Some examples from field experience indicate that the study of tribal culture—their mind, imagination and the customs which are followed for years-helps in planning and implementing schemes.

Village Development Boards in Nagaland

The VDB (Village Development Boards) in Nagaland were based on the idea of the Common Fund Programme and the committees constituted for the purpose were the Common Fund Committee(s) which was alternatively called VDB. This was built around the concept of "common belonging" which the villages in Nagaland know traditionally. The purposes for which a citizen may use the common belonging and for which these should not be used is well known to all Nagas. The idea of a "command fund" for development was just added to the list of common belongings, and it could properly strike and catch the imagination of the people. Any complaint from the Common Fund Committee would be placed before the Village Council. In every village of the Nagas there is a traditional Elders' Council. This Council, in official terminology, was called Village Council and entrusted with the function of resolving any grievance of a citizen or complaints from the Common Fund Committee. Its primary task was thus of a judicial nature. The whole thing was kept aloof from bureaucratic encroachments. On local people's demands the Deputy Commissioner was made the Chairman, but he only scrutinised the Committee's resolutions authorizing withdrawals or expenditure. Otherwise his role was a nominal one and ensured that power struggles didn't crop up in a village. For all other purposes the Village Council worked freely and enjoyed autonomy.[3]

Another example may be given of the primitive tribes, the Madia-Gonds from Maharashtra. They were averse to many new machines and innovations brought by development administration in the package of schemes. It was, however, intriguing to see that they accepted the tube-wells and used the water for domestic use. After studying their mythology it was known that they had a folk-tale according to which one of the forefathers from a clan prepared a big iron nail, tied a rope to it and with full force threw it in a particular direction. The big iron nail was thrust deep in the ground and a spring of water came up. The people then got water. Probably this analogy with the tube-well digging technique caught their imagination and they could accept the technology.

Tribal Culture in Folklore*

The undercurrent of Indian culture is the same throughout India. Tribal communities living in different habitats away from each other also display similar characteristics. They have still preserved—more or less—the cultural traditions which reflect their totality of life and an identity. Social organization based on kinship, clan system with

* This part of the chapter is contributed by Dr. (Mrs.) Shailaja Deogaonkar.

exogamous relationship at clan level and endogamy at sub-tribe or tribe level, an elaborate scheme of local and clan deities, nature worship, ancestor worship and animism which characterize tribal religion are presnet in all tribes with slight variations. Many rituals which may be connected with rains, sowing or harvesting operations, life-cycle rituals such as birth, marriage or death and celebrations of festivals are also common though their timings and forms may differ from tribe to tribe and place to place. Worship of trees in general and its significant presence in the form of *Mund* (pillar) which is of *Salai* (Bosvellia serrata) in most of the tribes underlines some basic integration in the classical culture of these tribes. Shifting cultivation and other forms of economic pursuits are also similar though not the same.

In its broadest sense tribal folklore encompasses all traditions, beliefs, customes, sayings, stories, etc., preserved among a community. This folklore which is a mirror of their culture is expressed in their folk-literature which is transferred from one generation to the other by oral transmission. The folk-songs and folk-tales constitute the bulk of this literature and are sung as songs on certain occasions. Singing and dancing go together on the rhythm of the beating of drums and other instruments which are usually made locally. Dancing and singing is common but is a must on festive occasions and ceremonies like marriage. It is a community entertainment. These songs are also collectively sung and "danced" near youth dormitories like the *Ghotul* in Madia-Gonds, or the *Morung* of the Nagas. Traditional political institutions of many tribal communities are still functioning very effectively and resolving local issues and problems with a method based on censensus. The egalitarian relationship and structure still exists. Hence development administrators must study and know the springs of tribal culture which are often contained in tribal folk-literature.

Culture is a term which is used by different scholars in differing contexts, usually all that which is non-biological and socially transmitted in a society including artistic, social, ideological and religious patterns of behaviour, and the techniques for mastering the environment is included in culture. It is also supposed to be the sum total of the attaintments and activities of any specific period, race or people, including their implements, handicrafts, agriculture, economics, music, art, religious beliefs, traditions, language and history. MacIver and Page are of the opinion that culture is something that a people crave after or need badly. A picture, a poem, a drama, a motion-picture film, a game, a philosophy, a creed, a cathedral are brought into existence because the people want them. They are the product of responses to a necessity within the folk, not to an outer necessity. Thus, these authors feel that the realm of culture is a realm of values, styles, of emotional attachments, of intellectual adventures, etc. It is the expression of our nature in our modes of living and thinking, in our everyday intercourse, in art, in literature, in religion, in recreation and enjoyment. Culture is tradition which is handed down by generation to generation. It is the "way" the people behave in a society. Language is the most important means of social transmission. Consequently, language is not only the medium of expression and communication between people but also a vehicle or a medium through which cultural transmission takes place. Wissler has given nine basic culture traits which give rise to culture pattern, wherein he gives first place to speech and language.

The opinions regarding culture can best be understood, if we consider the term culture as a conceptual system; which the anthropologists use to explain social behaviour. Michael, Silver Stein compare the conceptual system called "culture" to the conceptual system called "Grammar", which is used by the linguist to explain linguistic behaviour. He further says that grammar is a part of a culture. Both these are manifested only in society. The author maintains that the pursuit of anthropological studies, without the use and investigation of the native language of the people being studied, is unthinkable in theory, although all too frequently the case in practice.

All over India, tribal culture is broadly similar and has been a matter of great interest for foreign as well as Indian anthropologists. The material aspects of tribal culture include their food, clothes, ornaments, tattooing, utensils, housing, carvings, sculpture, traditional implements, musical instruments, paintings, etc. The spiritual aspects include the myths and mythology, religion including animism, social organization including the phratries and clans, totem and totemic clans, their conception regarding the unknown powers, superstitions, black magic, etc. A combination of material with the spiritual is implicit in the life-cycle rituals like those concerned with birth, marriage, death, etc. The fear and worship of the moon, the sun, the earth, trees, rivers, mountains and even animals exhibits their projection of the spiritual and the unknown in the material world with a view to get good life. The songs, dances, music are not only the expressions of pleasure and happiness, but also the explicit expression of culture. Their mythology and conceptualisation about the unknown, and spiritualization, is contained in the folk-literature which is in the form of songs which are orally transmitted from generation to generation. Even the ordinary experiences from daily life covering the problems, the sorrows, the joy and the ecstasy form the subject matter of these songs. The more "backward" the tribe, the richer its folk-literature. They have less inhibitions and hence the vent to the sentiments and ideas is profuse and free. Even the mythology is contained in the stories which are narrated in songs, which are sung mostly on a community basis, but rarely by individuals who are entrusted with the function, like the *Patadis* from the Pardhan tribals.

Lenin has rightly said that folklore is a material about the hopes and yearnings of the people. So as to study tribal societies one must know the folk-literature which is a mirror of their culture-past and present. Maxim Gorky has rightly said that one connot know the life of the people without studying their folklore and songs.

The tribal languages which are not only an instrument or expression of tribal culture, but even the carriers of culture, are usually in an oral form and are termed as dialects. In primitive tribal life the dialect serves a basic purpose, viz. expression of emotions and sentiments, mostly as a response to natural and social environment and the basic need for communication necessary for existence. Hence the styles, intonations, the sound or phonetics and the verbal sounds which are the symbols (later forming words) are all natural expressions. Consequently, the original tribal dialect is more natural though unsophisticated, and hence, alive. It serves the basic needs and slowly develops with the developing needs. The sounds in nature like that of the animals or of the rivers, etc., are adopted. This is how onomatopoetic words enter these dialects. The style of life (which is very slow and sluggish) influences the intonation curves which are often elongated. The dialect does have a grammar, a particular structure and forms of expression. Being oral, these may not be well developed but sub-serve the need of society. With changes in environment and life the intonations go on changing and the language also adopts intonation, style and even words from other predominant languages in whose contact the tribal population often comes. The process of acculturation is primarily through the process of acquiring and adopting the words and expressions through the more highly developed culture. In fact a word is a symbol of a cultural concept which may be either in a modified form or in toto. That is why it is often observed that for certain things or actions, there are no particular words in tribal dialect and they are adopted from another language. This is because the thing or the action itself is exotic to that tribal culture. Most of the Indian tribal dialects lack script as they continued through oral transmission. Among other anthropologists Prof. C. Von. Furer-Haimendorf who is an authority on many Indian tribes has advocated the use of "*Devnagri*" script for writing tribal languages.[4]

Tribal folk-literature can be broadly classified under four heads: Folk-songs, Folk-tales, Folk-drama and other types.

Folk-songs

This is the most popular form of tribal folk-literature and is associated with every aspect of life and with all occasions. The songs are in perfect metre and are mostly composed extempore befitting the occasion. When sentiments over flow, tribals have no dearth of expression. The words may change from place to place and from person to person. In those tribal communities who are still less acculturized, dancing and singing is a daily exercise of the boys and girls, joined by elderly men and women on particular occasions. Wherever, there are youth dormitoies (e.g. the *Ghotul* in the Madia-Gonds) the boys and girls assemble and dance till late in the night.

Two typical characteristics can be identified for the folk-songs, viz. they are normally sung while dancing. Tribals cannot sing the songs unless they start dancing. Thus, body movements, rhythm and verbal expression go together. Secondly, it is a community entertainment in which all participate. There is no distinction like performers and spectators.

These "dance-songs" (as we prefer to call them) are a product of individual authorship and also of communal authorship. Usually one person leads and others repeat, and this goes on repeating with much joy and mirth overflowing in the group. Musical bells, (*Ghunguru*), flute, drums (*Dholaks*), trumpets, etc., are played by the participants which provide melody as well as rhythm. Special or traditional dresses, headgears, costumes, ornaments, flowers, feathers of the peacock and other birds are profusely used by the dancers. The dances go on throughout the night, specially when the dancers consume indigenous liquor (*Todday* or *Mahua*) before the dance. Hundreds of items constitute the subject-matter for the song, like praise of God, welcome to guests, teasing each other, describing nature, sentiments concerned with marriage, love between lovers or spouses, brave deeds of forefathers, mythology, etc.

Folk-tales

These tales are narrated by the elderly persons to the youngsters or are sung as songs by the minstrels or religious leaders like *Pujari/Perma/Bhumka*, and so on. They are also sung in the usual dance sequences on certain occasions. These tales mostly contain the history of the tribe – mostly social and cultural and in some tribes the brave deeds of the kings and warriors from the tribe, creation of the universe, mankind and the social order in their tribe also find place in such songs. Some popular tales may also appear in this form. The unknown forces of nature are a source of curiosity for a tribal mind and the folk-tales attempt to interpret such phenomena, for example, there are tales explaining the creation of the sun, moon, fire and so on. The *Dhemsa* songs ceremonially sung by the *Patadis* (Pata means a song) among the Pardhan tribals contain the tales of *Lingo* and *Jangubai* – the saviours of the tribe and are common to the Gond and Pardhan tribals.

Folk-Drama

Folk-dramas are mostly ritualistic or historical in nature. The *Khamb* in the Korkus is a costume drama where men put on costumes of Gods and the role-playing continues. *Dandhar* is also a folk-drama common in tribal as well non-tribal rural populations. The *Gaon-bandhani* (fortification of the village through rituals) appears like a ritualistic drama among the Kolam tribals. The *Dussehra* function at the palace of the Maharaja of the Gonds at Aheri appears like a social-cum-ritualistic drama with costume and a lot of fun-fare and dancing at Aheri in District Gadchiroli.

A modern development among the tribals is the actual stage performances of small one-or two-act plays written by educated tribal youths and staged in the tribal track during festivals in which tribal boys and girls play different roles.

Other Types

These include assorted items like phrases, idioms, quizes, hymns (*mantras*) abuses (coarse revelry) and the utterances of *Shamans* while in a trance. At times one is surprised to note the imagination, intelligence and wisdom and the literary content in such items. The tribals are not shy of uttering abuses, as observed in the *Phool-jagni* function of the Korku tribals.

With modernization the new generation of tribals is drifting away from the tribal dialect and culture. Only the older generation still has a treasure of tribal folklore. It is essential to collect and record the literature before it vanishes from the tongue and memory of our tribal brethren, we cannot afford to forefeit this valuable stock of literature presenting a culture rich in qualities of heart and mind. The author has been able to study and collect tribal folk-literature of the Gonds, the Pardhans, the Korkus, the Banjara and so on.

REFERENCES

1. Mutatkar, R.K., *Socio-Cultural Dynamics of Tribal Life* (Special Issue), Tribal Research and Training Institute, Pune, 1990, pp. 19-20.
2. Knabe, Wolfgang K., "The Role of Sociology and Anthropology in solving problems of Indian Tribals" Paper submitted at a Seminar organized by TRDC. at Amravati.
3. Gokhle, A.M., "Village Development Boards in Nagaland", Paper submitted to the National Seminar on Nehru and Evolution of Tribal Policy in India, Sept. 1989, New Delhi.
4. Deogaonkar, S.G., (Ed.), *Problems of Development of Tribal Areas*, Leeladevi Publications, Delhi, 1980, p. 171.

9

APPROACH TO EDUCATION, EXTENSION AND SOCIAL WORK IN TRIBAL AREAS

THE percentage of literacy is extremely low ranging between 10 and 16 in the tribal areas and 0 (zero) and 5 in the primitive tracts. In the case of tribal women it is lower than 5 and in many areas zero per cent. Hence, when we think in terms of bringing awareness, functionality and functional literacy we are thinking in terms of adult education for the sprawling tribal populations and particularly those (above 15 or 18 years of age) who don't have an opportunity of schooling and formal education. Non-formal approach is adopted for such mass education programmes. Here, the programme has to be of the nature of continuing education and must have a nexus with adult education.

A Non-Formal Approach*

Education is, really speaking, a natural human phenomenon and a life-long process. Man has been learning for thousands of years through work and experience gathered while working for himself and his brethren. In the modern age, we take delight in fixing patterns or models which are considered as the standard ones for our modern life and the best suitable for the whole society. This so-called idealization of fixed forms of education may be useful (which again is debatable) for the urbanized society but is definitely less suitable for the rural population. According to the accepted concepts, rural education should be oriented towards agricultural pursuits. It is

* Based on an article written by the author and published in Vanyajati (Vol. XXVI, No. 3) July 1978, BAJSS, New Delhi.

concerned with all programmes including adult education, agricultural education and community improvement projects as working on farms or in villages. This can include domestic arts, instruction in basic facts and skills needed in their daily lives. In short, the curriculum must be based on the concrete and practical rather than on formal, abstract and theoretical aspects.

The nearer the population is to "nature", the greater is the need for increasing emphasis on the *functional* aspects of education. This applies squarely to the education of tribals. In most of the developing countries with backward or tribal populations, such approach is being adopted increasingly. Examples are available in the *nucleos* in Bolivia, the community schools in the Philippines (*barrios*), the tribal schools in Iran, the tent schools of the nomadic tribes in Ethiopia, etc. One common feature of all these is the priority given to the development of basic skills and knowledge in a manner which respects the particular culture and the initiating of community improvement at a pace acceptable to the community. Thus in tribal areas education must be a constant inter-action between school and community, a cooperative programme that utilizes the skills, the abilities and the efforts of the entire citizenry towards the improvement of community living.

In India we have been planning and implementing the Community Development Programme and we have travelled from the Special Multi-purpose Blocks for tribal areas and the TD Block pattern suggested by the Elvin Committee to the latest ITDP. But unfortunately even in a country like ours which had the fortune of having Mahatma Gandhi's ideas on basic and community education, his approach has not been put in to practice. Gandhiji used the term Gram Sevak to describe a village teacher which indicates his approach to education. But in the working which we have witnessed so far, neither the village teacher works like a Gram Sevak, nor does the Gram-Sevak perform the role of a village teacher.

In a scheme of non-formal education many agencies other than schools have a role to play. Examples can be given of the Community Welfare Centre in Ncora, Africa; the Himayat Sagar Extension Centre in Hyderabad, the regional fundamental education centres of the UNESCO in Mexico, the UAR, etc. This type of work includes teaching and leading the adults, helping them in finding solution to their economic and social problems so as to bring about improved agricultural practices, sanitation, health, literacy, service to homes and communities. The lessons drawn from the type of work done in the UAR, Korea, the Philippines, Puerto Rico, etc., and elsewhere indicate that the following three important factors must be remembered, viz.

(i) Recognizing the cultural factors in the community;
(ii) Involving people in learning to help themselves; and
(iii) Respecting the opinions of those affected, i.e. the beneficiaries.

While teaching adults one must remember what Firth said, that "people tend to respond more easily to stimuli which have some continuity or analogy with their traditional values". Specially while dealing with tribal adults it is important to do the following things:[1]

(1) Study the people and identify oneself with them;
(2) Initiate new ideas among them;
(3) Link ideas with their own local institutions;
(4) Touch the soft core of culture, first, essentially the material aspects, and them cover the humanitarian and service aspects of administration; and
(5) Try to win their confidence.

"Polyvalent approach" to education[2] also considers the varied educational needs—cultural, civic, spiritual, psychic, even political and others. An individual is studied and syllabii are adjusted according to his tastes, needs, aspirations, aptitude and environment. This flexible approach keeps opportunities for development open to the people throughout their lives. Integration of courses with inter-disciplinary nature, informal get-togethers, cultural programmes, etc., would get priority. Timings, venues, etc., would be according to the convenience and interest of the beneficiaries. Examples are Bombay Shramik Vidyapeeth, or Grameen Vidyapeeth in Rajasthan. In tribal areas this polyvalent approach can be adopted in Ashram School complexes and Growth Centres as starting of a Vidyapeeth may not be possible and viable everywhere.

Seva Mandir, Udaipur, a voluntary organization, has been working in the field of adult education and rural development. It has been actively working in Kherwara tehsil of Udaipur district for the past many years. The programme is an agriculture-based functional literacy programme covering about 80 villages through 100 functional literacy centres. The instruction at these centres was imparted by local educated youths who were farmers by profession.

Continuing Education in Tribal Area

The conference on Continuing Education in the tribal areas which was sponsored by the University Grants Commission and hosted by the Gujarath Vidyapeeth at Ahmedabad (in February 1978) stressed, among others, the following points.[3]

(a) Education and development must go hand in hand;
(b) The educator must identify himself with the people;
(c) Need for purposive and action-oriented research in the problems to guide the programme;
(d) Non-formal education should not get formalized but should be kept flexible enough to adapt itself to the changing needs and requirements of the tribal people and their environment;
(e) Education of the tribals must begin with arts and crafts that can add to the productive power of the concerned tribe;
(f) The content should be relevant to the environment of the tribe and the medium should be the language or dialect of the tribe;
(g) Conscientization and self-identity by the people restoring their self-respect and dignity is necessary; and
(h) The programme should be undertaken on a continuing basis.

Dr. T.B. Naik has observed that adult education has spread in the tribal areas,

(a) near the growth centres;
(b) where there have been other inputs including the infrastructure;
(c) where voluntary agencies have worked among the tribals;
(d) where the tribals have involved their own people to work with them;
(e) the teacher hand-books have been prepared in the tribal

dialects; and where

(f) the education has been related to the vocations of the tribal people.[4]

Teacher and his Methods

For teaching and leading tribals the teacher-leader must be a good student. He has to start with learning their language so that he can communicate easily to win their confidence and establish rapport. The tribal people must accept him as a man after which they can accept his ideas. Secondly, he must study their culture and social organization. This can even feed-back many good things to the teacher's culture as they (the tribals) have yet preserved many good things in their culture. To the extent possible the teacher must live a simple life similar to them. After knowing their problems and opinions he has to chalk out a minimum programme and try to secure their participation in its implementation. The new methods of teaching seek to develop skills, impart useful information, inculcate positive attitudes and provide a maximum of carryover to life situations. Building simple sanitary latrines, digging soak-pits and constructing bath places, smokeless *chullas*, keeping animals in good corrals, obtaining a pure-water supply, digging wells, widening and levelling of roads and digging drains on road sides, growing fruits and vegetables on farms or in the courtyards of huts, repairs to huts and to structures in public places (e.g. to *Ghotuls*/youth dormitories, Panchayat huts etc.) teaching improved agricultural practices, digging and filling the compost pits in a proper manner, childcare and hygienic living—this and many others represent items through which the worker gets opportunities to put education to work on the people's fundamental problems. This is extension education through social service.

Experience obtained in teaching adults throughout the world has following conditions.[5]

(1) Adults will learn only what they feel a need for. They learn best when they expect immediate benefits and when knowledge or skills will be directly useful in meeting a responsibility.
(2) Adults learn by doing—the importance of active participation in the learning process is greater among adults. They learn only about 25 per cent of a lecture, 50 per cent of what they learn in

one year will be forgotton and 80 per cent in two years' time.

(3) Adult learning centres on problems, and problems must be realistic. Let them begin with special problems drawn from experience and work out practical solutions from which principles may be deduced.

(4) Adults learn best in an informal environment. They will respond to adult programmes in inverse relationship to the degree they are reminded of their childhood experiences.

(5) Experience affects adult learning. New knowledge must be related to, and integrated with the accumulated results of a lifetime of learning experiences.

(6) Adults favour a variety of teaching methods. Learning proceeds more quickly among adults when information reaches the learner through more than one sensory channel (reading, direct contact, news article, radio demonstration, field trip, movies, group discussions, etc.)

(7) Adults want guidance not grades. They want to know how they are doing. They should be encouraged to measure their own progress.

(8) Experience shows that the training process should be based on the fundamental principle that people learn through seeing with the eyes, hearing with the ears, saying with the mouth, and doing with the mind and hands, and retain approximately as follows:

10 per cent of what we read
20 per cent of what we hear
30 per cent of what we see
50 per cent of what we see and hear
70 per cent of what we say
90 per cent of what we say and do

It is *doing* which makes learning permanent.

Researches on the development of tribal communities have established that education has a positive relationship to change in other spheres of socio-cultural and economic activities. So as to change the attitudes of adults, adult education can work as a carrier of attitudes. But adults would accept and react favourably to education programmes if they are non-formal, continuing, productive and useful and relevant to real-life situations and problems. The problem is more delicate and challenging in tribal communities. Thus right approach and careful planning of the methods and techniques of adult education programme assumes great significance.

Social Service

Field experience of working with tribal communities for social service and other developmental activities based on present experience indicates that the priorities of the programme should be[6] –

(i) Talk their language/dilect,
(ii) Stop their exploitation (cultural and economic),
(iii) Organize them locally and provide an *indirect leadership* which develops local leadership through a "snow-ball" process,[7]
(iv) More employment through local-produce-based cottage and small-scale industries, and better wages;
(v) Organizing them in local, social organizations with accent on games and sports, dancing and signing;
(vi) Community action for getting their local problems solved (for which traditional institutions still exist in tribal communities), with a "tribal-culture-touch" but tuned to a slow switch-over to a new life.

All this can be done if we adopt the most suitable methods and techniques of extension. Changing their orthodox attitudes towards life is important. *Method* and *result-demonstration* planned to suit the local problems have proved to be the best methods for tribal areas. Exemplary patience and adjustment with local circumstances are expected from the worker who must know and appreciate the richness and good points in the tribal culture and be ready to accept and learn such aspects leaving behind his prejudices. It is necessary to gain knowledge, skills and attitudes through real-life experiences and, based on these, transfer the knowledge skill/techniques or ideas by making them[8] *learn* to do, *do* to learn, *earn* to live, and *live* to develop.

Another programme which can attract and enthuse the tribal people towards a life-long process of education and prosperity is through more production – both agricultural and industrial.

Experience of an anthropologist-cum-tribal social worker in the North-East Indian region indicates that while introducing new ideas, enterprises, it is better not to plan or insist (at least initially) on a very ambitions programme but go slow and follow the line of least resistance particularly in the sphere of culture.[9] In fact, a Minimum Achievable Programme (MAP) should be chalked out and operated modestly. A peer group formed of the local youths/workers may pilot and operate the programme. This was successfully tried by Sewa Mandir, Udaipur, in Kherawada tehsil of Gujarat and also by the Tribal Research and Development Council in the primitive tribal areas of Etapalli tehsil in Gadchiroli district of Maharashtra.

While working for development, material aspects of life should be tackled first. Economic aspects, better roads, agriculture, stopping of exploitation, employment, health services, etc. should be taken up first. Never interfere with their religious ideas or rituals. Even removal of superstitions should come later, after their confidence is won by developing other facilities. Appropriate technology based on local natural resources should get priority. Some examples are utilisation of solar energy, bio-gas and gobar-gas plants, tube-wells with hand pumps, contour bunding and mud dams, identification and use of medicinal plants (tribals already know herbal medicines, hence they can be of help in this scheme), smokeless-*Chullas*, soak-pits, compost manure pits, woodcraft, carving, metalcraft, tanning and leather work, etc.

The richness of their culture and all the good aspects in their traditional institutions should be respected and openly appreciated. "Big-brother" attitude must be give up. An anthropologist-administrator or an administrator with orientation in the culture of the tribe can work well for development at both planning and implementation stages.

For workers working amongst the tribal people a rewarding programme is of conscientization of the tribal people which leads to the rise of their self-confidence, self-respect and awareness of the potentials within them. This leads to an end of fatalistic attitudes and serendipity. They can rise to all occasions and face problems confidently.

Audio-visual aids yield good results in tribal education or extension. Film shows, television and video can be used with good response. Pictures, photographs, wall posters, etc., can be displayed on festive occasions and fairs. Extension in health and hygiene, childcare and nutrition, mother's care, prevention and cure of diseases, anti-addiction drives can be very well organized with these methods. Appropriate technology and awareness about science can also be imparted through these methods. Television sets with disc antenae in tribal areas was a good technological in-put with good prospects for tribal education but failure in follow-up and maintenance resulted in non-use of the sets. Good schemes like bio-gas, gobar-gas plants and for the use of solar energy for street lights, etc., also failed just due to the apathy of the operation departments. Social workers can play a positive role in such situations.

REFERENCES

1. Haldipur, R.N., "Emerging Tribal Leadership", in *Development Administration in Tribal Areas*, H.M. Mathur (Ed.), HCM State Institute of Public Administration, Jaipur, 1976, pp. 33-34.
2. Hooja, Rakesh, "Polyvalent Education for the Tribals", *Ibid*, pp. 151-153.
3. U.G.C., New Delhi, Report of the Conference on Continuing Education in Tribal Areas, Feb. 25-27, 1978, p. 9.
4. *Ibid*, p. 5
5 Sanders, E.N., *Importance of Human Side in Farmers' Training*, Note presented as USAID Extension Advisor (Training) to the Directorate of Extension, Ministry of Food and Agriculture, GOI, quoted in *Administration for Rural Development in India*, by S.G. Deogaonkar, Concept Publishing Co., New Delhi, 1980, pp. 152-153.
6. Deogaonkar, S.G., *The Madia of Bhamragad*, Inter-India Publications, New Delhi, 1982, p. 105.
7. King, Clarence, *Working with People in Communities*, Case Records of Community Development in Different Countries, Harper, New York, 1958, p. 20.
8. *Ibid* p. 41.
9. Standefer, Roma L., Cultural Problems in Development of Small-Scale Industries in North-East India, Paper presented to the Xth ICAES, New Delhi, 1978, p. 4.

10

ETHNOGRAPHIC NOTES ON TRIBES – GONDS, BHILS, SANTHALS, NAGAS

The Gonds

The Gonds constitute the largest tribal group in India and spreads over a large geographical area. They appear as the main population of a wide area in the heart of India, described usually as the Gondwana. It spreads from the gorges of the Godavari in the south to the Vindhyas in the north. From the north bank of the Godavari, Mahanadi and its tributaries, the Narmada, the Wardha, along with the Wainganga and Pranhita rivers, the Eastern Ghats and the Stapura including the Maikal hills constitute the Gondwana. A few are found in Orissa and on the borders of Gujaret.

In Andhra Predesh they are found in Adilabad district and in Chandrapur and Gadchiroli districts of Mhaharashtra bordering with Andhra Pradesh. They are also found in Yovetmal district, Kinwat tehsil, parts of Nagpur and Bhandara districts. A large population of the Gonds is found in Madhya Pradesh, particularly the Satpura plateau including Betul, Chindwara, Chhatisgarh region, Seoni, Mandla, Bastar and Jagdalpur areas. As per the 1971 census they were estimated to be 5.8 millions.

Though there are cultural variations in the Gonds found in all these areas, they speak Gondi or deviation of Gondi dialect and consider themselves as Koitur the universal equivalent of that name in all Gondi dialect. In the Telugu area they speak Koya while in Madhya Pradesh their dialect is mixed with Hindi. Gondi with its local dialects is a Dravidian language akin to Tamil and Kannada and to Telugu.

The different regional groups among the Gonds are identified with different names which appear like the sub-groups of the great Gond tribe. The Raj-Gonds, the Koitur/Koya, the Naik-pods, the Dhurve, the Khatulwar Gonds, the Marhia/Madia Gonds, the Muria, the Hill-Marias, the Bison-Horn Marias, the Parajas, etc., are all Koya/Gondi speaking sub-groups of the Gonds. In fact, ethnically, culturally and even linguistically the tribal group recognized as Pardhans is also a castaway ethnic group of the Gonds and is given a lower status below the Gonds. The Marhia/Madia, the Muria and Bison-Horn Maria are at low levels of acculturation and are classified as "primitive" in some parts.

The Gonds have phratries of clans which are based on the number of Gods worshipped. There are Four-God, Five-God, Six-God, Seven-God groups called Yerwen, Sarven, Saiven Nalven respectively. Rarely a Twelve-God group (called Torey) is found. These are all exogamous groups. There is endogamy at sub-tribe and tribe levels but exogamy at phratry clan level. Clan names are totemic, though totem is not practised by the Gonds.

The Gonds are nature worshippers and practise animism. Ancestor worship is common. *Persapen* worship is common among all the Gonds. Goddess Kankali/Ankali is also worshipped and the local forms and names may vary from place to place. *Lingo* is the chief saviour and his legend tells about their social organization. The legend of *Jungobai* is also present in different forms in different regions. Gond mythology is prolific and tells about the origin of their tribe, its migration, etc.

For all life-cycle rituals like birth, name-giving, puberty, marriage and death there are elaborate rituals with celebrations, offerings to gods, accompanied with feast, drinking of liquor, singing and dancing.

Traditionally, there is no child marriage among the Gonds and girls are married after reaching puberty. Bride-price is practised which is mostly paid in kind and in lieu of it the groom renders service to the girl's father for predetermined period. He is then called a *Lamajanya* or *Dhaglya*. Polygyny is common and two or three wives are common. But in modern days this is receding. Divorce is common and is granted by the Panchayat. Widow remarriage or remarriage of a divorcee is permissible. Women have freedom in selecting life partners and can take initiative for divorce. The status of women is quite high except for participation in religious rites.

The Gonds bury the dead though burning of dead bodies is not a taboo. In the Marhia/Madia, Bison-Horn Maria, Muria, etc., stone slabs are erected as memoirs for the dead which are called *Kalbanda* or *Menhirs*.

Superstitions are common. Magic is also practised for warding off evils or black magic against the enemy. The class of priests called *Pujari, Perma* or *Bhagat* is common. They perform rituals, propitiate gods and spirits of the dead and may also offer magical cures. Some *Permas* have good knoweldge of herbal medicines.

Seasonal ceremonies and offerings are common. Before sowing seeds, at the time of harvesting and while eating the first produce, etc., *Poojas* are offered which are mostly on a community basis. Feasts with liquor mostly *Toddy* or *Mahua* are common on such occasions. The festivals observed include Dussehra, Diwali and Holi. Respect and offerings are presented to their traditional Maharajas on the Dussehra day which shows their links with the erstwhile feudal kings of the Gonds.

The main occupations of the Gonds include agriculture, picking up of minor forest produce, working as labourers on farms or in forest, and minor occupations like smithy, metal work, goat-keeping, piggery, etc. With education and developmental schemes they have entered other occupations and vocations. In the primitive Gond tracts in the Gadchiroli (Maharashtra) and Bastar (Madhya Pradesh) areas shifting cultivation is still practised on the slopes of hills, though it is now on a very small scale. Gonds in these tracts grow minor millets like *Kodon, Kutki*, etc. By and large the Gonds are rice eaters and eat all non-vegetarian food, excepting beef. In the primitive Gonds milching cows, buffalos and drinking milk was traditionally tabooed, but of late they are using milk. Fish is consumed by them and in the wilder parts they eat all reptiles and birds. Hunting is now nominal due to forest laws.

The Gond culture is an ancient and classical culture which is reflected in their folk-literature. Youth dormitories are common and among the primitive Gond tribes of Gadchiroli and Bastar the youth dormitories called *Ghotul* are still functioning. Young boys and girls assemble, sing, dance and choose their life partners. Transmission of culture and accumulated wisdom of the tribe through songs is also done in the *Ghotuls*.

The Gonds appear prominently on the political scene of past centuries—unlike any other aboriginal people, and also as a ruling race equal in power and material status to many contemporary Hindu princes. The first Gond forts were built in Manikgarh (Chandrapur), Surjagarh and Garh-Mandla. They had conquered the Mana Kings in Chandrapur. Later they also conquered Nagpur and other places. The building of forts marks the beginning of feudal power among the Gonds. Originally it was an egalitarian society without political hierarchy but with the advent of feudal power political power predominated, but still social equality was maintained including the feudal king or Maharaja who was treated as equal on social and other ceremonial occasions. This is also supported by the fact that there is no specific word for "king" in the Gondi dialect. The Gond Raja of Chandrapur and the Aheri Zamindar are still respected by the Gonds.

Songs are composed extempore and are sung while dancing. Theirs is a community entertainment. Men and women of all ages participate. Beating of drums (*Dhols*), musical bells (*ghunguru*) and other instruments are used. Dances and songs are specific for occasions and on festivals. Drinking of Toddy or Mahua precedes all such occasions. On the occasion of marriage and festivals like Dussehra, Holi, etc. dancing on community scale is common. The teenage boys and girls assemble near the *Ghotul* and dance daily in the evening. Songs replete with mythology and knowledge about their culture, forest environment, etc., are learnt at the Ghotul. Some songs contain folk-tales and Gond mythology. Other songs contain themes classified according to the occasion. The *Relaa* dance of the Madia-Gonds and of the Bison-Horn Madia is very popular. The more acculturized Gonds don't have dancing as a regular feature. But on occasions like marriage they call the *Patadis* (singers from the Pardhan tribe) who sing the songs called *Dhemsa* which contain the mythology of the Gonds. This has ceremonial as well as religious significance for the Gonds.

The Bhils

Bhils are considered to be a colarian tribe associated with the Munda group of tribals. It is the third largest group of tribes in India. Their habitat is in the hilly tracks of central India, Madhya Pradesh, Rajasthan and Gujarat. It spreads to the Khandesh area in Maharashtra and to the west from the Satpura ranges to the sea in Gujarat. Etymologically the word "Bhil" is considered to be derived from the word *Billu* meaning a "bow", as, traditionally, the Bhils used the bow and arrow and were warriors. Later, many Bhils took to robbery. They are also experts as hunts-men. Dholka in Rajasthan is considered by them as their ancestral home. As per the 1971 census they are estimated to be 5.2 millions.

The Bhils worship Hindu deities and many other local godlings. *Shravan-Babdeo* is their tutelary village deity. They worship Lord Mahadeo and in Maharashtra the Bhils also worship *Khandoba*, the war God of the Marathas, considered as an incarnation of Mahadeo. They are animists and worship hill, tiger, serpent as deities. They observe Dussehra, Diwali and Holi festivals. Though some Bhils were forcibly converted to Islam by Aurangzeb, they continued their animism and worship of Khandoba. Some have accepted Christianity.

The Bhils are divided into two *hagas*, which include brothers, cousins, clansmen and the wider circle of the *hagas* on the paternal side, and *hagawadia*, i.e. marriageable relatives. Marriage between two *hagas* is not permissible, i.e. there is endogamy at the *haga* level. Polygyny is common. Widow remarriage is not permitted except with husband's younger brother. Bride-price prevails among the Bhils.

They have totemic septs. The number of septs reported ranges from 27 to 36. Examples are *Jamania* (jamun tree), *Rohini* (Rohan tree), *Avalia* (Amla tree), *Mori* (Peacock), *Solia* (sun), *Sanyan* (cat), *Ghodmarya* (horse killer), etc. In Rajasthan (Banswara district) 54 clans (*Jati*) have been identified which are exogamous. Some are reported to have 150-162 sun-clans.

The Bhils had their Bhil kings and some of them had been well known. Some brave Bhils revolted against the foreign rule. For example, Tantya Bhils (1878-89). The Bhils have a record of serving under the Maratha rulers and the kings of Gujaratha (Gujarat) and Rajputana (Rajasthan) who appreciated their bravery.

The Bhil villages are usually on mountain slopes and are known as *Pal*. Each *Pal* has many huts and the headman is called *Gameti* (a distorted form of Grampati.) In some areas he is also called *Vasavo*. This is a hereditary post and he is obeyed by all. He settles disputes and propitiates God. Caste panchayats are still active and consulted in settling disputes, marriages, cases of divorce, adultery, etc. *Vartanio* or Kotwal is an important functionary who performs rituals connected with death in the presence of the Bhils from the village and this assembly of villagers is called *Kol Padshah Mandal*. The

Pujari or priest of the village performs all religious rituals and magic. He also works as an attendant and runs on errands.

Traditionally, the Bhils were food-gatherers and practised shifting cultivation. Large grazing lands are owned by their village community. They live a community life and help each other. Cattle-farming and agriculture are common occupations. They also work on farms as farm labourers and on other works. Bonded labour is also common. They are liquor addicts and drink Mahua.

Their dialect is called *Bhilli*. It is a mixture of words appearing from the *Mundari* (Munda group) and Dravidian languages. However, it is mainly derived from Gujrati and is influenced by Marwari, and Marathi in the Maharashtra area.

The Bhils cremate their dead.

The Santhals/Santals

The third numerically most important tribe is the Santhals of Bihar, Orissa and West Bengal. This is one of the major Indian tribes with concentration in Bihar. They are in large numbers in Santal Pargana district of Bihar and are also found in Hazaribag, Singhbhum, Dhanbad, Purnea, Bhagalpur, Saharsa, Monghyr and adjacent areas. They belong to the Kaularian group of tribes and are akin to the Mundas in some respects. Now they are settled on the plains, though earlier they preferred to live in the hilly and forest areas. As per 1971 census they are estimated to be 3.6 million.

The social organization of the Santhals is based on four divisions, namely, *Kaskuhad*, *Murumhad*, *Saranhad* and the *Marudihad*, which may be broadly equated to the kings, priests, soldiers and farmers respectively. Thus it sounds somewhat similar to the four *Varnas* among the Hindus. There are 7 to 12 totemic septs among them which are exogamous. Opinions on numbers are different. Marriage within the Sib is also tabooed. Cellular as well as extended family patterns are found in them. They have about 100 totemic clans.

Among the life-cycle rituals of the Santhals, initiation ceremony for the young boys is a typical one. As a token of initiation, a burn-mark is given on the left arm by the burning tip of a country cigar. This marks the admission of the youth to society and social status.

Marriages are by free choice of the boys and girls. Marriages are of six types:

Kiring Bahu –	most common method in which mutual negotiations are done and bride-price is settled.
Ghardi Jawae –	When the bride's father has no son, the groom is required to stay with the bride's father.
By Service –	the boy serves at the father-in-law's place.
Kiring Jawae –	when the girl has a secret affair with the prospective groom, help in the form of money or cattle, etc., is given to the groom for starting new life.
Itup –	Out of a love affair; a boy just applies a vermillion mark on the head of the bride and demands her hand; later he has to pay the bride-price as settled by the village chief-Manzhi.
Nir-bolok –	the bride takes the initiative and enters the groom's house, facing all opposition from the groom's parents.

The poor people simply bring the bride and place a *Sindur* mark on her head, avoiding all ceremonies. The marriage is performed at the groom's house.

Widow remarriage and divorce are permitted. Widow remarriage is called *Sanga* and a *dimbu* flower smeared with vermillion is just stuck on the bride's hair-do by the groom. Widows are entitled to half the bride-price.

Divorce is possible if the couple agrees to it. They then just tear a *Sal* (Shorea robusta) leaf into two, signifying separation. Whoever of the spouces is at fault, has to refund the bride-price to the other in full. Levirate and sororate are also practised. Women enjoy freedom and authority in family like other Hindu women.

The Santhals cremate the dead. They believe in life after death. They immerse the burnt remains of the dead in the river Damodar which is considered sacred by them.

Like the Mundas, the Santhals consider *Singbonga* as their supreme god, who is considered the Sun-God. They worship many other gods, the next important being the *Marang Buru*. The important village goddess is the *Jaher-era* from whose name the Jaher-Khand (*Zarkhand*) party took its name. They also worship Lord Shiva and Durga from the Hindu deities. Animal sacrifices to Gods and Goddesses on festivals and ceremonies are common. Like many other tribals they believe in omens and magic. *Naike* is the village priest who performs rituals assisted by *Kudam Naike* who assists him in propitiating sprits.

The Santhals still continue hunting, food-gathering, fishing, etc., which are traditional pursuits. They also practise agriculture and produce minor millets, *tilli*, paddy and pulses. Rice beer is prepared in every house. Mahua is also consumed. Bows and arrows made of bamboo and wooden or iron arrows are used for hunting. Battle axes and spears are also used. They weave their cloth.

The village organization is perfect which controls the community. *Manzhi* is the hereditary village headman and stays at *Manzhithan* which is situated at the centre of the village. He holds land which is free of rent and collects rent from the villagers for which he gets small commission. He gives consent to marriage negotiations for which he receives liquor and a few rupees. He heads the Village Council and settles village disputes. His assistant, who also holds the post in a hereditary manner, is called *Jog Manzhi. Pramanik* is another official whose post is also hereditary. He holds rent-free land and officiates during the absence of *Manzhi* and is assisted by *Jog Pramanik. Jag Manzhi* is the controller of morals. *Naike* is the village priest and receives giran as remuneration from villagers. *Kudam Naike* is his assistant. *Gorait* holds rent-free service land. He works as a messenger, convenes meetings, conveys decisions of village officials and gives publicity. He carries out or implements directions like giving possession of land, etc.

Inheritance is like in the Hindus – the sons get a share, and women have no right in the movable or immovable property.

The Santhals have a system of showing social displeasure against person(s) committing heinous crimes like incest, grave crimes, gross indiscipline against village officials, etc. This is called *Bitlaha*. This is social excommunication or out-casting. Commutation is allowed except in offences like incest or eating food from "untouchables", etc. The penalty may be giving a feast to the community, payment of fines, slight physical torture like slight burning of tongue, etc. If such commutation is allowed he gets back his social status and privileges in society. With modernization the practice of *Bitlaha* is decreasing or is modified though not completely abondoned.

Superstitions prevail among the Santhals. Offerings are made to the dead souls. They believe in magic and magic-cure. A medicine man and a Bonga doctor are called to cure sickness. Before constructing a house they tie a roaster to a peg and if it survives for five days the site is considered auspicious for the house.

Totemism is present in the Santhals. Their totemic clans (numbering about 100) are named after plants, animals, mountains, rivers and many animate as well as inanimate objects. Many taboos are linked to totems.

Dancing is common and men and women participate. They dance in circles, and women clap with hands. Musical instruments are not many. Flute and *Tumdok* (drum) are used. Stringed instruments are also used.

The Nagas

The Nagas are ancient inhabitants of the north-east border areas. It is a mountainous region and their villages are located on slopes. Their habitat extends from the north-western extremity of Kachar to the border of Chittagaon. The area on the north-east frontier of Assam is known as Naga Hills area or Nagaland. Ethnically they are considered of Mongoloid origin. They speak different dialects of Tibetan or Burmese origin. As per 1971 census they are estimated to be 0.5 millions.

The sub-tribes of the Nagas include Angami, Sema, Mao, Konyak, Maring, Lahota, Kubai, Aao and Tangkhal. All of them have their own dialects, traditions, deities, etc. Every sub-tribe is known for its typical pattern of costume which is of bright colours. The Nagas were originally divided into two groups in the "kilted" and "non-kilted" and the former (kilted) included only Angamis (which means unconquered). They were distinguished by their dress and methods of cultivation. All other groups were covered under the "non-kilted". The angamis are animists, worship trees, water, ponds, rocks, etc., and believe in a supreme creator.

The Nagas are a warrior race and possess weapons, which, like dresses, are different in different Naga tribes. They used to have blood feuds and fierce fights reminding of savagery. As a tradition, the warriors used to wear the hair of slain enemy or a special collar on taking the first head. After head-hunting they also used to carry the skull as a trophy.

Savagery apart, the Nagas had attained a high level of culture. Though some Nagas practised *Zhum*, i.e. shifting cultivation, they had better knowledge of cultivation as compared to other tribes in the area. They also prepared coarse cloth from bark, cotton and woollen fibres, with artistic patterns and colour. Naga *Tartan*, i.e. a woollen *shawl* with black and red stripes was used as a mark of authority by the village chief. Their weapons which include a short knife "Dao", and spears are also hand-made and beautifully decorated.

The Nagas have a patriarchal family. The women enjoy almost equal status and can influence decision.

The village organization of the Nagas is typical. Villages are located on steep slopes of mountains and are fortified, by ditches and barricades on the inner side of the entrance and ridges on the steep-hill sides. The real basic unit is *Khel* which is a sept and is exogamous. They are all brethren by blood and are together while fighting wars with the outside world. Each *Khel* lives in one locality, i.e. village, and as such a *Khel* and not the village, is the basic unit of their social organization. About 500 houses are found in each village having a traditional habitat for centuries. Due to diversity in their dialects inter-communication between villages was scarce, which explains blood feuds.

The Aao Nagas who are more tradition-oriented had small village republics and had democratic traditions. The headman had nominal powers and all men behaved kindly with each other. They had a system of age-groups of equal age exercising authority for some years and then giving it to another age-group. The Angami Nagas have a Village Council with participation of all the elders in it. The Sema and Konyak Nagas are known for their strongly monarchist traditions. The Konyak Nagas worship the head of the community. The Sema and Konyak were ruled by hereditary chiefs. In some sects the villagers elected the village chief called *Gaonbura* (the grand old man as chief). He was given a *Tartan* by villagers as a mark of respect and authority. However, except the Sema and Angami Nagas all others had some form of democratic tradition.

Some typical institutions of the Nagas include the *Genna* the *Morung* and common village belongings.

Genna means a special form of worship to propitiate spirits, and it also means abstaining from work either for a festival or due to some calamity in the village. In short *Genna* is a community action. Strict rules are observed during *Genna* and all assemble in a community house called *Ka Ki*.

Morung is a community institution comparable to youth

dormitory. It is believed that the condition of a *Morung* indicates the condition of the village. Socialization process starts here for boys/girls at the age of six years. There are separate *Morungs* for boys and girls. They are taught duties, traditions through folk-tales and tales of heroic deeds of ancestors and warriors. Thus it serves as a civic school for the community. The inmates sleep in the Morung. Asylum is given in the Morung. Nothing is stolen from a Morung.

Common action and "common belongings of the community" for doing some socially desirable action for the community is their typical characteristic. All villagers contribute to it.

11

POLITICAL ORGANIZATION AND ADMINISTRATION IN TRIBAL SOCIETY

POLITICAL anthropologists have tried to identify the political sphere of tribal societies. Ambiguity is considered as a basic attribute of political power. Irrespective of whether they conform to tradition or bureaucracy, all regimes express this ambiguity. In tribal societies wherein even the social structures are intermixed, it is almost impossible to identify and define political structures. As a result, some anthropologists were tempted to classify same primitive societies as "Stateless Societies" as against the "State Societies". The political sphere is implicit and not explicit in such primitive societies and as such anthropologists like M.S. Smith reject the classification as "Stateless Societies". The important bases for defining the political sphere include spatial or territorial organization. Sir Henry Maine, Lewis and Evans Pritchard give importance to this aspect. The other basis is the functions which are performed. Internal security, internal cooperation for subsistence and survival and protection against external attacks are some of the basic functions. All the functions of the modern state are performed but are in a rudimentary form. Giving an example of the Eskimo Community Almond and Powell describe a situation in which the adult members from the community sit near a fire in the evening in an informal manner and discuss the offending behaviour of an individual and decide on punishment for him. A person may be designated or someone may volunteer to punish or even to kill the offender. In this process all the functions of a political system viz. adjudication, enforcement of decision, etc. are being performed; but the roles are neither specialized nor crystallized in specific structures or institutions.

The early political organization centred around kinship or lineage units, or ritual power. A headman or a Shaman may play a diffused role combining religious, economic and political roles. In the segmentary lineage system a number of autonomous kinship or lineage units, from the same tribe may form self-governing units, and in case of a conflict between them an *ad hoc* "political" machinery rises for resolving the conflict. In a pyramidal set-up chiefs and sub-chiefs represent layers of authority. The patrimonial systems are more centralized and are hierarchical in nature.

Basis for Organisation

As referred to earlier, kinship plays an important role in organization. In different forms of politico-territorial groupings, local groups based on kinship form the bases. Traditional or hereditary chieftains arise from such kinship groups and exploit the blind following of their kinsmen for maintaining power as well as prestige.

Territory is an important basis for settled political groups. They may have a geographical organization into villages, townships, districts, etc. The degree of autonomy may vary from group to group within the geographical sub-divisions of the territory.

The widest recognized political unit/group among the primitive societies is the tribe. A tribe may consist of different political units, although possessing a comman tribal culture, for example, the Naga tribes in India. On the other hand a political unit may cut across several tribes or may encompass several ethnically related tribal groups, for example, the erstwhile Gond Kingdoms of the Central Indian Highlands. The Munda and related tribes have also been found bracketed in political units. Common ethnic origin may be one of the reasons for forming one political unit. On the other hand several tribal political units may have a confederal type of organization with equal and autonomous units under a superior cental and legal authority which may work for common interest like defence of ritual celebrations. Among the primitive peoples like the aborigines from Australia a common religion may create a strong community wider than a political unit. Thus, whether they are of a uniform culture and of a homogeneous ethnic origin or not, if there is a well-developed central authority exercising final legal, administrative and military power over a group of people occupying a clearly defined territory, we have a "State" and a people as a "nation". The forms may differ from place to place and may be less or more developed.

In simpler societies, elders councils are more common. There is no formal chief and the unity of the tribe is ensured through rituals and ceremonies or through common action during fights with other ethnic groups. Warrier leaders emerged during such events but had a temporary character. In same political units there were chieftains simulating "Kings" who represented a centralised authority. As against this pattern there was a horizontal distribution of political power in local chiefs and local elder's/Village Councils.

Administrative set-up

We have discussed the various stages and forms of political organization in tribal communities. Depending upon these forms we can identify different forms and structures for administration in these societies. Functional specialization and distribution may vary from tribe to tribe depending upon the level of acculturation and stage (s) of development. Egalitarian relationship within the community is a characteristic of many tribes. Prof. C. Von Furer-Haimendorf says that among Gonds the segmentary organization based on clans and their phratries (groups according to the number of God-groups) was primarily a means for the regulation of marriages and for the *Persapen* worship, and it lacked a territorial base. Later, with the emergence of feudal stage it obtained a territorial base which led to a political basis. In his famous book, the *Gonds of Central Indian Highlands*, Dr. B.H. Mehta states that the stage of settling down on territory and the building of forts was an important stage of political organization in the Gonds and marks the beginning of feudal power in the Gonds. The first ever forts of the Gonds came up at Manikgarh near Chandrapur and at Garh-Mandla near Mandla. In fact there is no synonym for "king" in the Gondi language/dialect and except while discharging functions as their chief, he occupies equal status to any other Gond in their society. Both as a feudal chief and as a chief of army during wars he enjoyed a status higher than the headman of a village or chief of a clan.

Political Organization of the Gonds

The mainland of Gond habitat is traditionally known as *Gondwan*.

This was divided into three states: (i) Garh/Gad Mandla – North Gondwana; (ii) Deogad and Nagpur – Central Gondwana; and (iii) Chandrapur – South Gondwana.

On, the Northern slopes of the Satpura mountains Kherla was a Gond State. During A.D. 1247 one Kol Bhil established his influence in the Sirpur, Manikgarh areas near Chandrapur. The erstwhile power of the Deogiri Yadav Kings in this region was nearing its end. Even the rule of the *Nagwanshi* Mana kings had ended. Kol Bhil who was a Raj Gond, captured the fort from Mana kings and crowned Bhim Ballal Singh of the Atram clan the first Gond king.

Since then kings from the same Atram clan continued to occupy the seat of power

Administrative set-up

The Gond king of Chandrapur was also the highest authority of the Gonds of the Adilabad area (now in Andhra Pradeshh) not only as king or political chief but also as a tribal chief. He used to preside over the Panchayats in which disputes which could not be settled by the local cheifs were resolved and settled. Even after the Gond kingdom was abolished he held the same position as a tribal chief in matters pertaining to rituals, purification, social problems, etc. and his declaration prevailed in all such matters. This continued upto 1941, i.e., during the days of Raja Akbarshah.

Though the Gond Kings were (and still continue to be) from the Atram clan, their subordinate authorities were from other clans. These lower kings/chiefs included *Maharajas, Zamindars, Rais, Thakurs*, etc., and came under the military power of the Gond kings.

Thakur(s), the local chiefs, collected and deposited money as revenue and supplied army when needed. They maintained law and order, kept watch on criminals, could impose fines and confiscate property.

The organization in the Gond kingdoms at Chandrapur, Deogad and Nagpur was much similar. The officers entrusted with revenue collection also included Deshmukh, Deshpande, Huddar, Muharir and Varhadpande. However in the Gond kingdom of Chandrapur the *Zamindar* was more powerful and enjoyed a status akin to the king for his zamindari area. Under the Gond Kingdom of Chandrapur the Aheri zamindari was most powerful and still functions and gets the respect of the Gonds and the Madia-Gonds who are primitive, and inhabit the forest of the Aheri zamindari area (now covered in the Aheri, Etapalli and Sironeha tehsils of the present Gadchiroli district in Maharashtra).

The Aheri Zamindari

During the regime of Gond king Ramshah at Chandrapur, two Sardars under him, viz. Sadho and Mula, started a mutiny against the king. The king sent his relative Kokshah who killed Saho and Mula and got hold on Surjagad. The king gave the, *Zamindari* of the area as a gift to Kokshah who established his seat at Aheri. This happened in 1703 A.D. Since then the zamindari was establised. Kohshah was from the Sedmake clan, but from A.D. 1871 the zamindari passed on to Dharma Rao (I) who was from the Atram clan. The last zamindar was Dharma Rao (II) who continued till zamindari was abolished in 1950. Since then the Aheri zamindar continued to hold power as a tribal chief and wields influence as the Gonds in the area, in matters pertaining to rituals, social issues, cultural matters, etc. and is the central figure in the traditional Dussehra celebrations. At present Raja Visheshwar Rao Maharaj is the zamindar at Aheri who is college educated and is a former Member of Parliament.

The Administrative Structure under the Aheri zamindar

↓

I. The Maharaja of Aheri – Chief of the Zamindari Area

↓

II. Adivasi Sabha Patti (Sub-unit) – Council (A unit of 50-100 villages each headed by a Sendhia or chief.)

III. Four Pattis:

(i) Laheri Patti
(ii) Venusagar Patti
(iii) Jaravandi Patti
(iv) Ghat Patti

↓

IV. Village – headed by a *Gaita* or *Patel*

Sendhia who was the chief of the *patti* was an authority in the religious and social spheres for the group of villages. He was the chief priest and judge of the *patti*. The office was hereditary. When the interests of a number of villages were involved appeals against the decision of a *Panchayat* or a group of *Panchayats* went to him and in such cases his decisions were final. The cases from one Sendhias *patti* were never referred to another Sendhia, and when such a case arose in 1909 a great conflict arose between two *pattis* which could be resolved only after the intervention of the Aheri Zamindar who brought about a compromise and peace.

In each *patti* are included 50-100 villages. Each village has a headman called *Gaita* (or, these days *Patel*). He also functions as a *Bhumia* or religious headman of the village. In majority of cases both these posts are held by the same person. This post is hereditary and his authority is supreme over the village or the group of villages under him.

The Panchayat is not a standing body but is called when required. On receiving complaints, the Gaita calls two or three elders (the number is not fixed) and they sit together to hear the parties and decide the case with the help of elders. Different elders may be called on different occasions.

Thus, each village has its own Panchayat composed of a few village elders and presided over by the Village Headman, i.e. *Gaita*. Each group of villages acknowledges the authority of the Sendhia, who is the court of appeal for difficult or intricate inter-communal disputes. The Sendhia's authority is confined to his own *patti* which is a compact country, sharply defined by geographical boundaries like a nullah or river or hills, etc.

Political Organisation in the Korku Tribe

The Korku tribals from the Melghat area (Dharni and Chikhaldara tehsils) of Amravati district in Maharashtra show an altogether different type of political organization. A typical feature is the absence of any hierarchical structure, and also the absence of a tribal chief. Traditionally they have a horizontal pattern of power distribution somewhat federal without a central authority to control it.

The "Kings" who ruled the Korkus were Rajput Kings or chiefs. There were *Jagirs* of Rajput chieftains at Susarda and Kot. The Korkus, particularly the *Movasi* sub-tribe, indulged in brigandage, raided the areas in the plains and paid a part of the booty to their Rajput chiefs as ransom. The *Chavdi* or panchayat was under their control. During the course of history these Rajput Jagirs ceased to exist and now there are no traditional cheiftains.

The only chiefs appear at the village level. The Patel functions as a village chief and gets priority on social occasions as well as rituals. The *Bhumka* and the *Parihar* wield supernatural powers which gives them status and assures obedience to their authority. The Bhumka acts as priest and gets priority at ceremonies, festivals, etc. He is considered a traditional community leader and a socio-cultural guide. The *Parihar* is visited with divine spirits as a mouthpiece.

The Patel, who is often a Police Patel and the Bhumka wield authority on the Village Community in social, cultural spiritual matters.

The Hill Korwa

This is also a primitive tribal group having their habitat in the Bagicha Block of Raigad district of Madhya Pradesh. At a height of 2,800 feet on the Vindhyadri mountain, they spread over mountainous tracts of Jashpur tehsil, touching Mahnai village which is near the Bihar border. These tribals have more concentration near Sanna. Ethnically they are a branch of the Munda tribe, and are akin to the Korkus.[1] There is some similarity in the political organization of the Hill Korwa and the Korku. Like the Korkus, the Hill Korwa also lack a hierarchical structure with a centralized authority. The Diwan of Khuria who was a *Zamindar* was respected by the Hill Korwa as king. He was a Rajput by origin, and was a Baghel Kshatriya.

The only tribal chiefs among the Hill Korwa can be found at the village level. *Mukhiya* was the village chief and was greatly respected and obeyed by all. He used to issue dictates which were assiduously followed by all. During the regime of the Diwan at Jashpur, the *Mukhiyas* were elected by villagers. Of late, there is no election and a brother or nephew of the old Mukhiya assumes the post. The *Panchas* from the village may also select a person for the post. He plays an important role in settling disputes.

The *Sayanas* (the wise) or the *Panchas* are selected from among the eleders from the village for settling disputes. But the traditional panchayat is not in vogue. It is an ad hoc arrangement. Mostly on

Thursdays, five elders (Sayanas) are called, who sit together and after hearing the parties give decisions.

Baiga is the spiritual chief who guides in social and religious matters. He is usually a man of character and is a well-informed person. He acts as a friend, philosopher and guide for the villagers and hence assumes informal leadership. The post is hereditary and goes to the son.

Mukhiya and *Baiga* are the two chiefs and at times the same person may hold both the posts.

The Kolam Tribals

The Kolam tribals have been classified as a primitive tribe and is culturally related to the Gonds. These are found in Yovetmal, Wardha, Chandrapur and Nanded districts of Maharashtra as well as in Adilabad district of Andhra Pradesh. Their localities are called *Pod (Poud)* which is either an independent village or is situated out side other villages. There is no centralized authority and a *Pod* may shift to other place in certain circumstances and establish an independant *Pod*.

Political Organization

The Kolam *Pouds* present a typical political organization. There is a Panchayat which is traditional and runs the affairs of the village. It performs organizational as well as judicial functions. Even today the Kolams believe more in their Panchayat for resolving disputes than the police and courts.

There are your functionaries in the panchayat viz, *Nekun* (Naik) *Mahajanyak* (Mahajan), *Karbhari* and *Ghatya*. They are elected on the *Chaitra Shuddha Pratipada* or *Gudhi Padva* day, i.e. the first day of the Hindu Calendar. All Kolams assemble at the *Chavdi*, i.e. the public hall, for meeting, and the office-bearers are elected by consensus.

The *Naik* is a powerful office-bearer who presides over the panchayat and is also the chief of the Paud. He also presides over or blesses all rituals, ceremonies and even cultural programmes like the *Dandhars*. He settles the cases regarding property, inheritance and his decision is final.

Mahajan is the vice-president of the panchayat and performs similar functions.

Karbhari acts as secretary of the Panchayat, collects dues, keeps accounts and makes suggestions to the panchayat.

Ghatya is a messenger-cum-multipurpose functionary. He collects fines, delivers invitations, announces meetings, etc. But the nomenclature comes from the word *Ghat* (a pot full of water) which is used in marriages and he keeps a watch on the *Ghat* at marriage ceremonies.

As a helper to these four office-bearer is *Bhumak* who works like a *Kotwal* and may be equated to a peon. He serves the community in the *Pod*.

Pujari (or *'Deokari/Supari/Ghusadi*) is a religious leader and takes initiative in rituals and ceremonies. *Songadya* or *Vetalak* (clown) works as a priest for solemnising marriages, tells about future and also entertains people as a clown.

There is no feudal, hierarchical or centralized authority or ruler of any kind among the Kolams. But the above local organisation still persists and functions in many respects.

A brief look at the political organization and administration among the different tribal groups including those which are at a primitive cultural stage indicates that the tribal communities in India have had their own machinery for maintaining the law and order as well as judicial function and a "council" used to function effectively with a few office-beares. A chief and elders were the repositories of power but were under the general supervision and control of the council and villagers. Even the feudal chiefs like those in the Gonds consulted and trusted local and regional chiefes who in turn drew their support and acted on the advice of the elders or the *Panchas* from the village. Thus village councils were the springs and source of authority and justice.

The Tribal Councils

The Ministry of Home Affairs, Government of India, in its report[1] published in 1960, refers to the findings of the committee on special Multipurpose Tribal Blocks. It describes the functioning of the traditional tribal councils in different parts of the country.

In Assam tribal councils functioned in Garo villages, and dealt with all disputes and differences among people. Their powers included maintenance of peace and order and settlement of disputes by simple tribal ways.

Among the Khasi tribals there is a *Durbar* (Council) consisting of all male adults of the village. These *durbars* directed and guided the whole social and administrative functions of the village. Their decisions were binding on all residing within their jurisdiction and disobedience was punishable with fines or expulsion from the village. Above the council were chief's courts who heard appeals.

In Andra Pradesh the Koya tribals had traditional panchayats. These were called *Kula*[2] *Panchayats.* The village is a unit of administration and its chief if *Pinna pedda.*[3] This is a traditional post which goes to his heir after his death, but the heir is elected thus combining the hereditary principle with democratic principle. The assembly of village elders elects the heir and if he is a minor or has some incapacity they elect a regent. Above him is a *Kula pedda* or *Patel* whose office is hereditary and is like a Munsif recognized by the Government.

A group of 10 or 12 villages forms a *samutu* over which is a *samut dora*, *kulu dora* or *pedda kapu* but is just a chairman of the council and is guided by the opinion of his colleagues. Appeals against the decisions of *pinna pedda* or *kula pedda* (Patel) lie before the *samutu*. *Pinna pedda* or Patel may also be fined. The fines (tappu) are of three types: payable to the community (Kulu Tappu), to the religious head (*guru tappu*) and to the head of the State (*Raja Tappu*). There is no king (Raja) and hence fines go to the *kulu* and are usually used for community drinking. If the fine (may be up to Rs. 100) is not paid social boycott may also be imposed.

In Orissa the Ho tribals have a different type of organization. The Hos elect a President called *Marang Gonke* from the villages of a particular area who is assisted by other headmen in regulating the religious and social practices of the tribe. The Council constituted of the village headmen from the villages in the area, fixes the dates of religious functions and marriages, dances and festivals. In matrimonial cases it hears the parties and prevents irregularities and may even impose fines. During the sixties it had taken up the question of abolishing dowry and had encouraged literacy. Annual meetings of headmen in the area are held under the chairmanship of the *Marang Gonke* and social affairs are discussed and directives issued. The headmen and the *Marang Gonka* are not hereditary posts but depend upon their continued influence or popularity among the people.

Tribal councils have been traditionally functioning in the NEFA area and have certain common characterisitcs. They derive their authority from ancient times and in fact, are the expression of the will and power of the whole people. They are supported by social and supernatural sanctions. All councils are informal in character, though some (e.g. Monpa councils or Bangos of the Adi) are more highly organized Community spirit and sense of unity is very strong.

The leaders of the *Kebang* in Siang (a council of the Adi) begins its meeting with the following recitation.[4]

> "Oh! Villagers and brethren, let us strengthen our customs and our Council, let us improve our regulations; let us make the laws straight and equal for all. Let the leaders who can speak best stand up and speak out for our betterment; let them speak out in a bold voice unabashed and undaunted like a cock crowing. Let our laws be uniform; let our customs be the same for all. Let us not decide differently for different persons; let us be guided by reason and see that justice is done and a compromise reached that is acceptable to both the parties. Let us keep nothing pending; let us decide while the dispute is fresh, lest small disputes grow big and continue for a long time. Let the fine be levied reasonably. Let it be commensurate with the guilt and be just. Poverty should have compassion and justice be tempered with mercy. We have met in the sacred place of justice; we have come together for a council meeting and let us speak in one voice and devide on one verdict."

With these words the council starts work and justice is meted out so that all those present are convinced that one who was right got it. Shri D. Venkatapayya who was an eye witness to many enquiries by panchayats said "... I have got great regard for the manner in which questions are logically put and answered and the enquiry done in a judicial manner and have no hesitation in saying that the panchayat system, as it now exists among the tribesmen, is a glorious survival of the ancient Hindu panchayats . . . , It has got a healthy tone for discipline over the entire community."[5]

The recitation quoted above shows that there was rule of law and equal justice for all. The process of administering justice was not delayed and they realized its bad effects. The idea to strike a balance between opposing interest of parties was present in their mind. The fines and penalties were proportionate to the element of guilt involved. The factor of poverty was also considered while deciding upon punishment. The tribal councils urged their members to speak out the truth without fear. These are principles which sound most modern and even warrant adoption by us.

Tribal Insurrections

In general the tribal people of India are calm, peace-loving and at times meek. Unless provoked, they don't fight. Except such tribes which practised brigandage as an occupation, others like the Gonds and many others did not use arms against outsiders. However, there are instances when they as a community or some heroes among them fought violently and bravely against outsiders. We may call them as uprisings or violent movements against exploiters or foreign rulers.

The name of Tantya Bhil has become legendary. He fought against the British regime and was active in Indore State, Elichpur, Hoshangabad area during 1878-89.

Umed Vasava, a Bhil of Panchdongri district, was one of the main figures in the unrest in Rajpipla state during 1873-1882. During the war of Independence of 1857, Tantya Tope was helped by many Bhils.

In Bihar the Bhumji Movement was started by the Santhals against the exploitation by landlords. It started under the leadership of Ganga Narain Santhal and was continued by Kandu and Siddhu Santhal, who during 1850 faught against the traders and landlords who exploited them. During 1897 Birsa Bhagwan Munda led a movement against exploitation which is well known.

In Orissa, the Khonds the Saparas and the Koyas started movements in 1879 and 1890 for getting their rights.

The Pahadi Reddis started a movement in 1879 for getting their ownership rights in lands.

The Oraon tribals started a non-violent movement under the leadership of Nana Bhagat against the British regime in 1914 for getting equal justice.

In 1910 the tribals from Bastar started an agitation in Madhya Pradesh for getting autonomy for Bastar state, but it proved abortive.

In 1940 the Gonds agitated under the leadership of Bhima Kumra Gond while the Koyas agitated under the leadership of Aluri Sitaram Raju in Andhra Pradesh.

During 1920, there was a Devi Movement in the Maharashtra and Gujarat regions. The Mungela Koli tribals started the movement. In the Vasai area women possessed with Devi (Goddess) moved in society and preached against non-vegetarian diet and consumption of liquor. The tribals were impressed and accepted it. It spread very fast in Thane, Nasik and Bharoch, Baroda districts. As a result tribals stopped working in Parsi households because the Parsis ate meat and consumed liquor. Thus this can be termed a social reformative movement.

In Dhule district of Maharashtra there was a tribal Saint Gulya Maharaj. He spread the message of the *Varkari* cult during 1930 and became popular among the tribals. He died in 1940, and his brother Ramdas Maharaj continued the movement. Later the movement turned against the officials of the Forest and Police departments who harassed and exploited tribals. Hence the movement was branded as a "political" movement and their religious prayers, *Aarti*, etc. were also banned. Ramdas Maharaj was asked to leave the district. He, later, worked for the rebabilitation of those who were displaced and had become homeless due to the Ukai dam project.

Godavari Parulekar organized a movement in Thane district of Maharashtra which lasted from 1945 to 1953 and is well known. She worked among the Warli and other tribas in the area and organized their movement aganist bonded labour, Begar (forced labour), etc. She organized conventions of tribals at many places against such practices. Shri Shyamrao Parulekar was asked to leave the district, The tribals discontinued working on the lands of *Zamindars*. Some tribals resorted to weapons and violence. The police started large-scale arrests. Thane district assumed the form of a war field. Though leftist in nature this movement was never under the control of any Communist Party.

Thane district in Maharashtra has been an abode for many tribal movements indicating a high level of tribal conscientization. After 1951 many lands belonging to the tribals were transferred to the non-tribals in spite of existing legislation banning such transfers. Shri Ambarsingh Suratwanti Maharaj started an agitation. This was concentrated mainly in the Palghar area of Thane district. Shri Kaluram Dohade continued the agitation after Shri Suratwanti till 1974 when the Government promulgated an Ordinance suitably amending the Land Revenue Code and Tenancy Act so as to rectify the situation. Similarly the tribals demanded that the Government regularize the encroachments on forest land by them for farming, etc. and grant them rights over such land. But the Government refused. Consequently, a federation of various tribal organizations was formed under the name of Jabaranjot Andolan Kruti Samiti which started a movement and the Government had to promulgate an Ordinance in September 1979, granting rights over such encroached forest land to the tribals.

In the Dahanu-Talasari area of Thane district an organization called Bhumi-Sena was formed which worked for the identification and emancipation of the bonded labour among the tribals under the Bonded Labour (Abolitions) Act of 1976. Even the tribal custom of asking the bridegroom to serve as a labourer at the brides father's place in lieu of bride-price (Lamanya or Lamjanya or Dhaglya system) was opposed by these activists.

Chandrapur and Gadchiroli districts of Maharashtra have a large concentration of tribal poplutaion. Gonds are the major tribe and in Gadchiroli district there are primitive Tribal areas inhabited by the Madia-Gonds, classified as a primitive tribe. During 1952 to 1972 Shri Narainsingh Uike, a tribal leader who was a socialist, worked in the Kurkheda, Dhanora area (now under Gadchiroli district) for tribal awareness and conscientization. He organized them for demanding land rights on encroached lands. Shri Sukhdeo Babu Uike continued the movement. In 1980 he established Jagrit Adivasi Sanghatna (an organization of vigilant tribals) and conducted awareness camps, seminars, conventions, for the tribal population in the area. The problem of wages, employment guarantee scheme, etc., were discussed. Camps for the study of herbal medicines in the area were also organised. Dr. Satish Gogulwar, who is an M.B.B.S. and is practising at Kurkheda, has organized camps and seminars of tribal Pujaris/Permas and experts from outside on herbs found in the area and their medicinal uses. He is associated with the organization and also conducts educational, social awareness activities. The Jagrit Adivasi Sangathana also organized a Jungle Bachao, Manav Bachao (Save jungle, save man) movement to oppose the big dams at Inchampalli and Bhopalpattanam on Maharashtra, M.P., Andhra Pradesh border. Taking the approach of environmentalists, these agitators protested against the probable ethnocide, destruction of forest, wild animals, plants, etc. and displacement of tribals from their traditional habitat and a general disturbance of the balance in the eco-system. Joga

Madavi, a local Gond leader, Mohan and others were prominant among the leaders of the movement. The Government had to rethink on some aspects of these dams.

The Inderveli movement in the Utnur taluq of Adilabad district of Andhra Pradesh in 1981 was remarkable in so fas as it was a spontaneous reaction to the grabbing of the lands of the tribals by non-tribals. An action committee was formed to take back such lands and thousands of tribals were invited at Inderveli for a large vonvention on April 20, 1981. The police, in a bid to disperse the tribals, resorted to firing. About 60 tribals (official figure quoted was 16) died in the police firing. The then Chief Minister, Shri Anjaiyah, had to go to Inderveli and he announced Rs. 10,000 as compensation to the relatives of the dead and Rs. 5000 each to those injured. The Government also promised to take steps so that all the tribals could get back the lands grabbed by the non-tribals. Thus the agitation succeeded.

The brief account giving information about a few tribal agitations/movements indicates that these erupted due to one or many of the following reasons:

(a) Cultural or religious reforms among the tribal communities,
(b) Moral or economic exploitation of the tribals,
(c) Land alienation by non-tribals,
(d) Historical processes including foregin rulers, and
(e) Defective or faulty implementation of development schemes, etc.

The Tribal Mind

A study of the tribal movements and a diagnosis of the causes helps us in understanding the tribal psyche and the reactions of the tribal mind. They have still preserved their traditional social and political institutions and the study indicates that the traditional Tribal Councils or Panchayats still have legitimacy and even credibility for the tribals. On the contrary, the statutory panchayats elected as per the prescribed legal procedure don't have the same credibility and do not enjoy the confidence of the tribals, though, at times, the same persons may be elected. The bond of and a commitment to the traditional institutions is firm and is considered as a pious duty. It is due to this reason that any interference with their social or political institutions is not tolerated. But if they are convinced about the efficacy and usefulness of the new idea or structure, they accept it whole heartedly. The development administrators must bear in mind this attitude of the tribal mind.

It may prove helpful to utilize the community spirit present in them through their traditional organizational structures rather than thrusting upon them the new patterns of administration. For the purpose of developing tribal areas multiple administrative agencies are functioning with a lot of over-lapping and duplication of effort. In spite of the scheme of democratic decentralization, the tribals could not be involved either in decision-making or in the process of implementation. It has been already suggested by the author in the fora concerned with the planning process that it is still possible to involve the traditional Tribal Council and their Village Headman in the development process. They are still in a stage in which they collectively utilize the products and services in their community. Rather than selecting individuals for the grant of benefits and creating a feeling of "haves" and "have-nots" and thus breaking their traditional community spirit, our Government which is committed to socialism should utilize the aspects of primitive socialism seen in the tribal communities. This may start by taking up community benefit schemes. Under the ITDP. There are schemes like ploughing of farms with tractors, building of "*Samaj Mandirs*" (community centres), digging of wells or small water tanks, construction of schools or *Anganwadis*, development of demonstration farms or horticultural farms, etc. All these may be entrusted to the traditional Village Council and the Panchas/elders and the Patel or Mukhiya of the village will get such schemes executed by utilizing to local communities' labour and cooperation. Only technical guidance required may be provided. Funds should also be kept at the disposal of the local council. Apart from ensuring the much talked of (but less achieved) people's participation in development, this will also reduce to the minimum the role of administrators and of course reduce the siphoning off of funds due to corruption. Even in the case of individual beneficiary schemes, the local council may decide the persons whom the benefit should go first. A sense of participation in one's own development will give a tremendous boost to the confidence and sense of honour of the tribal and they will not feel that they are treated as lower grade citizens by us. Peace will then come to the tribal areas along with development.

REFERENCES

1. *Report of the Committee on Special Multipurpose Tribal Blocks*, Ministry of Home Affaris, G.O.I., New Delhi, pp. 156-165.
2. *Kula* means Community
3. *Pedda* means an elder.
4. Elwin, Verrier, 1965, *Democracy in NEFA,* North East Frantier Agency, Shillong, p. 17.
5. *Ibid*, p. 6.

BIBLIOGRAPHY

Bhange, N.P.; 1993, *Tribal Commissions & Committees In India*, Himalaya Publishing House, Bombay.

Deogaonkar, S.G., 1980, *Administration for Rural Development in India*, Concept Publishing Co., New Delhi.

Deogaonkar, S.G., 1980, *Problems of Development of Tribal Areas*, Leeladevi Publications, New Delhi.

Deogaonkar, S.G., 1988, *Political Anthropology*, Kitab Mahal, Allahabad.

Deogaonkar, S.G., 1990, *The Korku Tribals*, Concept Publishing Co., New Delhi.

Deogaonkar, S.G., 1982, *The Madia of Bhamragad*, Inter-India Publications, New Delhi.

Deogaonkar, Shailaja, S., 1993, *Maharashtratil Adivasinche Loksahitya*, Shri Sainath Prakashan, Nagpur. (In Marathi)

Draft of the Eight Five Year Plan, Maharashtra State.

Elwin, Verrier, 1965, *Democracy in NEFA*, North-East Frontier Agency, Shillong.

Indian Journal of Public Administration. Selected Issues Five Year Plans—First to Eighth Plan Reports published by Govt. of India.

King, Clarence, 1958, *Working with People in Communities*, Harper, New York.

Mathur, H.M., 1976, *Development Administration in Tribal Areas*, The HCM State Institute of Public Administration, Jaipur.

Raghavaiah, V., 1972, *Tribes of India*, Vol. II, BAJSS, New Delhi.

Raha, N.K. Coomer, P.C., 1989, *Tribal India*, Vol. I & II, Gian Publishing House, New Delhi.

Reports and documents published by the Planning Commission.

Reports and other publications of the Governments of Maharashtra and Madhya Pradesh.

Sharma, B.D., 1978. *Tribal Development : A Brief Review*, Tribal Research and Development Institution, Bhopal.

Sharma, B.D., 1986, *Tribal Development : A Theoretical discussion* (in Hindi), M.P. Hindi Grantha Academy, Bhopal.

Vidyarthi, L.P., 1986, *Tribal Development and IFS Administration*, Concept Publishing Co., New Delhi, 1986.

Index